The 1904 Reviv

CW01511316

This is two books in o
eyewitnesses to the revival.

Book One:

The Awakening In Wales And Some Of The Hidden Springs

by

Jessie Penn-Lewis

****

Book Two:

The Religious Revival in Wales 1904

by Awstin and other special correspondents of the Western Mail, London, 1905

Great Plains Press, Lawton, OK

Edition 1.0, 2012

Library of Congress Catalog-in-Publication Data
Penn-Lewis, Jessie
Awstin

Title: The 1904 Revival in Wales
1. Revival 2. Christian history 3. Reformation 4. Welsh history

ISBN: 978-1461197270
Softcover

Learn about other books by Great Plains Press:
        www.greatplainspress.wordpress.com

Table of Contents

The Awakening In Wales And Some Of The Hidden Springs

By Jessie Penn-Lewis

****

The Religious Revival in Wales 1904

by Awstin and other special correspondents of the Western Mail, London, 1905

Note from the Publisher

These two books were written just after the turn of the 20th century in Wales; as a result, there are a few words that are not in English, but in Welsh, the original language of Wales. Also, those Welsh words could not be checked to verify their correct spelling. It also has European spelling of words which is sometimes slightly different from American spelling.

Great Plains Press

Preface

In the days of the primitive Church it was considered necessary that a full and authentic record should be written concerning the coming of the Holy Ghost, and all the mighty workings which followed His descent into the upper room at Jerusalem. When the right time comes such a treatise concerning the outpouring of the Holy Ghost in Wales in 1904-1905 will be found necessary, for Wales is "making history "—Divine history—these days. Doubtless, also, the Lord Himself is preparing a "Luke" for this service!

In view, then, of future history, it becomes the bounden duty of each one with authentic information to contribute his or her quota to the common fund. Such a duty lies on me because I have for the past few years been on the "watch-tower," watching the movements of God, and I may not withhold from the Church of God what my eyes have seen of His "mighty works" preparing and leading up to this awakening, which we trust and pray may be the beginning of the wider fulfilment of the prophecy of Joel.

The greater part of all that I have written in the following pages is from first-hand information, which has come in such a way that I could not fail to see the Lord directing it to me for the purpose of this story, and I am greatly indebted to the clergy, ministers, and others, who have sent me various accounts of the work, in some instances having to translate from Welsh to English— demanding no little labour and time in the midst of other pressing claims. I have thought it best to omit all names with the exception of those already publicly connected with the revival, although I recognize that in the days of Pentecost the story was told in all its simplicity of truth— with no thought of honour to the instruments of God as "they rehearsed all things that God had done with them."

To obtain a wide vision I have also sought to write from the view-point of the Mount of God. The Spouse in Canticles cries to the sister-bride, "Come with Me (and) look from the top." May we heed His call, and" ascend into the hill of the Lord," and "stand in His holy place," whence we may watch in the world" The voice of the Lord hewing out flames of fire," and "breaking the cedars." But it is obvious that the following pages cannot possibly unfold all that the Lord has wrought in the prayer-movement, or His inner workings in the Principality of Wales. Indeed, the story of His marvellous workings in each of the few centres I have briefly referred to would easily fill a chapter of themselves.

I have only placed on record what I know of some of the springs of the Revival—springs to a great extent hitherto unseen by the world, and I do this not only for the sake of future history, but because it is of the most vital importance that the people of God should discern the true inwardness of God's workings, lest they be occupied with the outward manifestations, and seek to copy that which only can be produced by God Himself when His people obey the conditions of blessing. With this special object in view I have chosen, out of the quantity of material in my hands, to record those instances of the working of God which emphasise the aspect I have enlarged upon in my last chapter, i.e., that God works from the midst of a Spirit-filled people out upon the world. If the "Revival Dawn" in Wales is to increase to noon-day power, all who long for world-wide Revival must see to it that they hasten the day by personally entering the Spirit-filled life, whilst congregations must seek—what may never have entered their minds before as possible—to have their "Pentecost."

As I close I cannot refrain from referring to a "romantic coincidence" which has come to me personally within the last year in the renewal of my childhood's friendship with Dr. Cynddylan Jones. As a girl of fourteen I was the little companion of Dr. Jones and my father, who together were convalescents in a Hydropathic Establishment near Bath, after serious illness. My father was taken to the heavenly home, and Dr. Jones was left to continue his ministry for God, little dreaming that the child who played around him in those days would, in later years, have the privilege and joy of linked service with him in telling the story of a great revival in their native land.

May the Eternal Spirit use the messages toward the fulfilling of His desire to lead the Church of God back to Calvary and to Pentecost. Then shall "the glory of the Lord be revealed, and all flesh see it together, for the mouth of the Lord hath spoken it."

Jessie Penn-Lewis
GREAT GLEN, NEAR LEICESTER, April, 1905.

Introduction

Wales is a land of periodic revivals. In the middle of the eighteenth century "a love coal from off the altar" touched the lips of Daniel Rowlands, a clergyman of the Church of England, and inspired him with a fervour which no opposition could quench. The genteel and respectable Christians of the period called him the "cracked clergyman" of Liangeitho. But if he were cracked, the Welsh nation has reason to be for ever grateful, for through the "cracks" he beheld God and Eternity, and the vision filled his soul with boundless enthusiasm. In a few years all Wales was ablaze. People from far and near came to witness the stirring effects of his preaching; the hearers wept and shouted, thus outraging all the proprieties. Did that marvellous Revival leave anything behind it of permanent value to the nation? Yes. First, as the Revival in England left behind it a new religious Communion, the great Wesleyan Methodist Church, so in Wales it created a new denomination, the Calvinistic Methodist Church, which in numbers, influence, and learning, ranks with the foremost of the denominations in the country. Second, it gave Wales its Hymnology. Till then the nation had no hymns. Now we have a heritage of hymns rich beyond compare. These hymns revitalised the religious life, and as a consequence the nation has moved on a higher level ever since. That movement in course of time expended its force. But in the beginning of the last century another Revival started. John Elias with his theological sermons, Christmas Evans with his poetical sermons, and Williams of Wern with his philosophical sermons, travelled the country, proclaiming the doctrines of grace, each in his own way, overpowering their hearers, throwing them into a religious ecstasy, and once again the large congregation shouted and sang with joy. All Wales was like a boiling cauldron. Gradually the flames of emotion died out. What was left—ashes? By no means; that convulsion in the spiritual experience of the population raised the national life to a higher level. Emotionalism? Aye; but it fed the roots of intellect, infused new life into the Tree of Knowledge as well as the Tree of Life.

However it be among other nations, in Wales the Life is always the Light. As the first Revival gave us our Hymnology, so the second gave us our Theology. Probably there were not men learned enough to write standard books of their own, but there were many able to translate the standard works of other authors. Accordingly, under the influence of this Revival, were rendered into the vernacular of Wales, Dr. Owen on the "Person of Christ," "Justification," and the "Work of the Holy Spirit "; Matthew Henry's Commentary, and a number of other Puritan books. Under its influence Bunyan's Pilgrim learned to speak Welsh on his journey to the Celestial City! In the absence of light literature, the farmers and the peasantry spent their long winter evenings pondering over these books, discussing their teaching in their adult Sunday Schools and their week evening meetings, with the inevitable result that they became thoroughly grounded in the fundamental doctrines of Salvation. Puritanism entered the blood of the Welshman, it still colours his every thought, and can never be expelled. Hence his aversion to rites and ceremonies—to all appeals to his aesthetic nature, and his readiness on the other hand to respond to all appeals to his spiritual nature.

In 1850 the enthusiasm of the former days had quite died out. Church life was placid even to torpidity. The elderly men and women were calling to mind the years of the right Hand of the Almighty, and sighing for a wee bit of a breeze. And in 1859 the third Revival broke out. Humphrey Jones, a young Wesleyan minister, catching the fire of the American Revival, crossed the ocean to convey the flame to his native land. He held prayer and preaching meetings; all the countryside in North Cardigan was talking of the young Revivalist. Alas! his bodily frame could not stand the strain, and in three or four months his nervous system broke down, and he could never face a congregation again. But he had not laboured in vain, for before his collapse he had imparted the fire to a neighbour of his, the Rev. David Morgan, a Calvinistic Methodist minister, a man of splendid physique. The transformation wrought in the latter was simply miraculous. That which I know I speak, for I was an eye-witness of it all. He toured the country from Holyhead to Cardiff, spoke as one inspired, towered high above all his compeers during the three years of his strange uplifting. Crowds hung upon his lips, the ungodly cried out in agony of soul, the saints shouted for joy—their noise was like the noise of many waters. All the country was aflame. It is computed that about 100,000 converts were added to the churches.

There were critics and scoffers then as now. "If, therefore, the whole church be come together into one place, and all speak, and there come in those that are unlearned or unbelievers, will they not say that ye are mad? " (1 Cor. xiv. 23). Literally, will they not say that ye are under the influence of a demon? That probably was the criticism of unbelievers on the revival in Corinth; that certainly was their criticism on the revival of rang in Wales! Fortunately there were others, more sensitive to spiritual influences, who replied, "Well, well, if this be the work of the devil, he must be a very new devil to Wales. The old one sent the people to the public-houses, the new sends them to the churches; the old made them dance and swear, the new makes them leap and praise."

By their fruits ye shall know them." Emotionalism, extravagance—yes; but they burnt out the old impurities. Wales was lifted high on the crest of that revival wave; when the wave subsided, what was left—froth? No, but higher aspirations after holiness and an intense love of learning. Since then the number of worshipping places has been doubled, thousands of schools have been built, and three national colleges established— all having their roots in the revivification of the religious life of nearly fifty years ago. The first Revival gave us our Hymnology, the second our Theology, the third our educational system, which competent authorities pronounce to be second to none in the world to-day. Every Revival, like the overflowing of the Nile, leaves a rich deposit behind to fertilize the national character.

That memorable Revival in the roll of the years spent its force. For the last ten years the spiritual life in our churches was becoming more and more depressed. Our best spirits were lamenting the impending lapse of our fatherland into barbarism. Earnest crying was made unto heaven. For months we felt there was a vague, indefinite, mysterious something in the air—a going in the top of the mulberry trees. The godly mothers and maidens were the first to feel the return of the tide, which for the last few months have swept all before it. The story of this fourth Revival will be told in the following pages by one in complete sympathy with all spiritual movements, and possessing the advantage of understanding thoroughly the generous impulses of the Celtic heart and the subtle windings of the Celtic brain. But I may be allowed to indicate two or three of its outstanding features.

1. It is independent of all human organisations – straight from heaven. Missions are revivals. Men can organise the former, not the latter, and it is a pity the distinction should be so often over-looked. Man's method of saving the world is by costly and complicated machinery-salvation by mechanics; but God's method is by vital energy-salvation by dynamics. "I am not ashamed of the Gospel of Christ, for it is the power, the dynamic, of God unto salvation" (Romans i.16). St. Paul, the missionary, relying upon prayer and the dynamic power of the Gospel, changed the face of the Roman Empire. And in Wales to-day all is spontaneous. The dynamite is

working, explosion follows explosion, and already scores of thousands of rough, hard stones have been loosened from the quarry of corrupt humanity, and where explosion frequent and powerful take place, is it to be wondered at that there is tumult and confusion? Better the confusion of the city than the order of the cemetery.

2. Much importance is attached to the work of the Spirit, at least in its initial stages. Heretofore the work of Christ has been the all-important truth, to the exclusion to a large extent of the doctrine of the Spirit. Much emphasis has been laid on receiving Christ, scant stress on receiving the Spirit. Now, however, the question is coming to the forefront, "Have ye received the Holy Ghost since ye believed?" (Acts xix. 2). There were thousands of believers in our churches, who like the disciples St. Paul met at Ephesus, had received Christ, but had never received the Holy Ghost. The mark of Christ's blood was upon them, but where was the mark of the Spirit's anointing? Saved themselves, they made no attempt to save others. The present Revival, however, whilst not obscuring the doctrine of the Cross, has brought into prominence the doctrine of the Spirit. Thousands of Christians, who had received the Christ, have now received the Holy Ghost, and as a consequence they are filled with the spirit of service—no task seems to them too hard for Christ's sake.

Whilst this doctrine is by no means new to theology, in the present movement it has assumed a new forms at least in experience. Orthodoxy has always conceded that conscience speaks within us; but in practice we have effected too wide a separation between conscience and the Holy Spirit. This Revival has again united these. " Something tells me to do this and avoid that," says the man. "Some Thing," answers the young Revivalist, "why don't you be honest? Why don't you say Some One? " And the Revivalist is right. A Thing can never speak. It is not Some Thing but Some One who speaks, none other than the Third Person in the Holy Trinity. Does not this invest conscience with grand sacredness? We all believe in the need of the Spirit to regenerate and sanctify—— to accomplish the great tasks of life, the works which we know no human power can effect; but alas! We are not in the habit of introducing the Spirit into the common acts of our every day life. But the Scripture teaches us to seek the Spirit's guidance in all things—He is the source of all prudence and wisdom.

3. The third feature is enthusiasm, a feature common to all Revivals. Many Christians who love gentility and moderation would like to receive the baptism of the Spirit without the baptism of Fire. But what God has

joined cannot be sundered. "He will baptize you with the Holy Ghost and fire " (Matt. iii. II); there is the verse—what will you do with it? There is only one preposition in the original, not two as in the English, to show the identity of the two baptisms, or rather that there is but one. Wherever the Spirit descends He brings fire in His train. "There appeared unto them cloven tongues, like as of fire, and it sat upon each of them. And they were all filled with the Holy Ghost, and began to speak with other tongues, as the Spirit gave them utterance." Hearts of Fire and Tongues of Flame. Is enthusiasm permissible in every department of life, but forbidden in church life? A thousand times, No. How speaks the Apostle ? "Fervent in spirit, serving the Lord." Fervent, literally, boiling. " Boiling in spirit." Let none be ashamed of "boiling" in the service of the Saviour. At all events I prefer the congregations that boil over to the congregations that will not boil at all. "The fervent prayer of a righteous man availeth much." Literally, the boiling prayer. The cold prayer even of a good man will avail nothing in heaven or on earth, but the boiling prayer of a righteous man has ere now performed wonders, and will perform them again.

How very cold and formal the prayers of the Church have been for many a long year! But for the last four months there has been everywhere a marked change—the prayers have been boiling and whole multitudes have been thrown into a state of extraordinary fervour. It rejoices me to see the rising generation boiling with a great enthusiasm in the service of Christ—the mark of the " boiling will be on them as long as they live. None are the same after boiling as before. Hundreds of our young men and women had been brought up religiously in the home and the church; but their religion was cold, format, following routine. Hardly any of them had courage enough to bow the knee in public; prayer, with the inevitable consequence that only aged men engaged publicly in the weekly prayer meetings.

Behold the difference! Now our young people flock to the services, prayers flow spontaneously from their lips like water from the spring, praise ascends to heaven like the carol of birds in spring. No forcing, no inviting— spontaneity characterises the proceedings from beginning to end. No one is ashamed of confessing Christ as his or her Saviour— rather the shame is on the other side. All the chapels are crowded, the valleys and mountains ring with praise. The following story will show how gamblers refuse money won by bets made before conversion, how prize-fighters are now soul winners, how thieves restore stolen goods, how husbands return to their deserted homes, how enemies are made friends. Scores of pages can be filled with as striking conversions as any in the annals of the Christian Church.

Do we justify the extravagances? Not more than Paul justified them at Corinth (I Cor. xiv.)! We know what they mean, are able to interpret the tongues. Out of the confusion will emerge order and beauty and life. All criticisms are met by the prophet's question, "What is the chaff to the wheat? " (Jer. xxiii. 28).

J. CYNDDYLAN JONES

1. The First Pentecost in Jerusalem and Joel's Prophecy

The Prayer-Movement - The Prayer-Circles in 1902--The Renewed Preaching of the Cross.

AFTER the tragedy of Calvary, and the magnificent Resurrection and Ascension of Him Who is now alive for evermore, the Ascended Lord sat down on the right hand of the Majesty on High, and received of the Father the "promise of the Holy Ghost" for His redeemed ones as the fruit of His Cross and Passion. He then poured Him forth upon the company of men and women gathered together with one accord in the upper room in Jerusalem—the city where He was crucified.

Giving them commandment "through the Holy Ghost," almost His last words to them before He ascended had been "I send forth the promise of My Father upon you: but tarry ye in the city, until ye be clothed with power from on high."

Returning from Mount Olivet to Jerusalem they set themselves to obey, and with one accord continued steadfastly in prayer until at last the day dawned, and the Holy Ghost came as the "rushing of a mighty breath."

The word used to describe His advent is significant. The breath of the Spirit is spoken of by the Lord Jesus to Nicodemus when He told him that men dead in sin must have a new birth—a birth from above which would come by the breathing of the Spirit of Life upon them, so that they are begotten of God. And "the Spirit breatheth where He listeth! Men could hear and see the effects as with the wind, but not know "whence it cometh and whither it goeth."

Later on we read that on the first Easter Day the Risen Lord stood in the midst of His disciples, and, showing them His hands and His side scarred with the marks of Calvary, breathed on them, saying "Receive ye," or, as it is literally, "Take ye the Holy Ghost."

We cannot doubt that the disciples received the Holy Ghost when the Risen Lord breathed upon them, but their immediate after-life shows that it was not the energising for service and clothing with Divine power, which the Lord so expressly bade them tarry for ere they attempted witnessing for Him. The breathing upon them of the Holy Ghost on the first Easter Day seems to have been the "earnest," or preparation for the Pentecostal fullness of the Divine Spirit, and they would have sorely failed to enter into His greater purposes for them had they said "But we received the Holy Ghost on the day of His resurrection!" and not waited at Jerusalem until they were "baptised in the Holy Ghost," or clothed with Him, as the Lord had promised.

But they obeyed and tarried, possibly scarce knowing what the outcome would be, until suddenly there came from heaven a "rushing mighty breath." The breath of God which gives the new birth to every believer, now came forth with such force and volume that it filled the very atmosphere of the house where they were sitting. The believers were now, so to speak, submerged in the Holy Ghost, as well as indwelt by Him. In this intensely surcharged atmosphere the Divine Spirit became manifest— apparently to sight as well as hearing—and there appeared unto them tongues like as of fire "distributing themselves," and resting upon each one present, until each—no matter what the temperament, education, training, position, sex, or age might be—" began to speak" as the Spirit gave them utterance.

The city of Jerusalem knew nothing of the little company quietly meeting and praying in the upper room! But now they could not be hid. Hearing the sound of voices the multitude came together, and saw the Spirit-filled company so manifestly under the control of some power which lifted them out of themselves that some said "They are filled with new wine," whilst all were amazed and marvelled, saying, "Are not all these which speak Galileans? "— untaught, uncultured people from the province of Galilee.

The world had been going on its way, ignorant of all that God was silently working in the spiritual realm to bring about the counsels of the ages.

But now! "What meaneth this? " cries the gathering multitude. Ah, momentous things had happened in the unseen realm, and all that had been wrought by the death of the God-Man at Calvary must now be made manifest to the world that crucified Him! The Third Person of the Godhead, the Eternal Spirit of the Father, comes forth to bear witness to the Crucified and Risen Lord, and clothe human beings with Divine authority as His messengers.

In answer to the charge of being filled with wine Peter rose to speak— the very man who just a fortnight before had denied his Lord in that same city. Speaking under the constraint of the Divine Spirit, he said, "This is that which hath been spoken by the prophet Joel:- "And it shall be in the last days, saith God, I will pour forth of My Spirit upon all flesh; and your sons and your daughters shall prophesy . . . . on My servants, and on My handmaidens in those days will I pour forth of My Spirit; and they shall prophesy."

Let us mark the words, for they vitally concern the people of God to-day. "This is that which hath been spoken by the prophet Joel," said the Apostle. Not "this is the entire fulfilment of the prophecy." It is written " I will pour forth of My Spirit upon all flesh," and this speaks of a larger circle than one hundred and twenty men and women. Yea, a larger circle than even the three thousand and five thousand souls, and "multitudes" more of men and women so quickly "added to the Lord." The words undoubtedly foretell a wider fulfilment of the prophecy than took place at Pentecost.

Joel said "in those days will I pour out My Spirit." The expression "is in the long Hebrew tense, expressing continuance of action, literally an incoming, unfinished, and continuous outpouring.' It therefore appears that the words " in those days cover the whole dispensation of the Spirit, beginning with the day of Pentecost. The purpose of God was manifestly a beginning in the upper room; and a continuing upon wider and wider circles as the overflowing stream of life reached the "uttermost parts of the earth "; but alas, alas, the Church, instead of abiding in a Pentecostal condition, drifted further and further away from it. Nevertheless the Word of God standeth sure. The Church shall be brought back to her Pentecost when she knows her need and turns to the Lord.

In the prophecy of Joel we see foreshadowed under the figure of "rain" the work of the Holy Ghost. Joel speaks of the Lord's response to the cry of His people, when He would cause to come down for them the "former rain " and the "latter rain", then AFTERWARD should come the outpouring of the Spirit upon all flesh, and a time of such manifestly supernatural workings of the Spirit, that whosoever would simply "call" on the name of the Lord should be delivered. The "former rain" was always given in Palestine to cause the seed sown to germinate and grow into maturity. The "latter rain" was looked for as essential to the plumping out of the grain for its ripening and fitting for harvest. How clear the forecast of the purposes of God toward His people in the Gift of the Holy Ghost.

We need not now attempt to trace the Divine movements in the world preceding the first Pentecost. Were we to do so, we should find them strikingly parallel with those in recent years, when the condition of the professing Christian Church has become similar to the Jewish Church at the close of the dispensation before the Messiah appeared.

It will be sufficient for us to emphasise that Joel's prophecy clearly sets forth the preparation of the people of God by a seeking unto God in prayer. We read that they are brought by His providential dealings to a consciousness of their need, and are summoned to leave all their interests, and with one accord to seek His face; then would come the Lord's response in overflow of personal blessing, and the pouring out of His Spirit in such measure that the world should be touched, and sinners call upon the Lord. The first Pentecost at Jerusalem exactly fulfilled this forecast. Bereft of the One Who had been with them in bodily presence as Teacher and Guide; faced with His command to go forth and disciple all nations; conscious of their powerlessness to fulfil this commission, and of their lack of position, culture, knowledge, and all the resources which would command the attention of the world to their message, the little company of disciples gathered with one accord to pray until they were equipped with power from on high.

PRAYER preceded the first Pentecost, and PRAYER must precede the wider outpouring of the Spirit in the last days, therefore the true members of Christ all over the world must be drawn by the Spirit within them into one accord in asking God to pour forth His Spirit according to His word. The extent of the one will govern the extent of the other, for prayer prepares the channels for the Holy Spirit to fill, and flow out through into the world.

The question therefore arises as to whether there has been in recent years any indication of the special preparation of the Church for the wider fulfilment of Joel's prophecy. If we find this to be so, our faith will be strengthened, and our vision cleared, to see that the Revival in Wales may be the beginning of the "latter rain" which shall prepare the Church of God for the Lord's appearing, and draw into the kingdom all who willeth to be saved.

To obtain a wide vision, let us in heart and mind now ascend into the secret place of the Most High, having boldness to enter the Holiest by the blood of Jesus, and look out with Him upon the world, and watch the movings of His Spirit among His people. We may only find the veil lifted here and there, and obtain but glimpses into His workings, but these will suffice to give insight into His preparations over the earth for the fulfilment of His purposes toward men.

We will go in thought back to the year 1898 or 1899, and glancing into an Institute in America see gathered there three to four hundred children of God, meeting every Saturday night to pray for a "world-wide revival." In this Institute we find men and women from every clime seeking equipment for the preaching of the Gospel. Their hearts yearn over their own lands, and "world-wide" must be the blessing which they seek. After a time a few began to stay in prayer late at night, and ceased not until the early hours of the Sabbath morning. Among them was one who was their Leader. Conscious that they who pray must be ready to be instrumental in answering their own prayers, he offers himself to God for any special service in the bringing about of the prayed-for Revival.

Rapidly we cross in vision to another far-away land, and in Australia find a band of ministers and laymen who have met for eleven whole years every Saturday afternoon, pleading with God for a "big revival." In the wondrous chain of the Divine workings, we next see a messenger called out from the heart of the praying company in America, to be one of the instruments in Australia, of God answering these prayers—the very one who had laid himself at the feet of the Lord of the harvest, ready for all His commands.

In 1901 we look into the great city of Melbourne, and see fifty missioners holding services in fifty different centres of the city, whilst 40,000 praying souls meet in two thousand homes for "home" prayer meetings, encircling the city with prayer. Many meet for half nights of prayer, and Melbourne is moved from end to end by the mighty movings of the Spirit of God.

We come again in swift thought back to Great Britain, and look in at the huge meetings of five thousand Christians gathered at Keswick in July, 1902. Hark! The story of the "home prayer circles" around Melbourne is being told. Hearts of workers are burdened and sad. Weary of organisation and effort, no fresh "Prayer Union" would appeal to them, but quickly the spark from the fire in Australia falls into many hearts. "Home prayer circles!" The "twos and threes" of those who are truly burdened for "world-wide revival!" Ah, this is the call of God! If a city may be thus girdled with prayer, why not the world? Quickly are the names of those who are drawn of God to pray sent in from all parts of the earth, until thousands of praying hearts were circling the globe with prayer. It is God's prayer union gathered and guided by Him, with no organization, no membership fee, no staff, but just the few who register the names as a labour of love for souls. And the prayer was now for the "outpouring of the Spirit!" In other words, a Pentecost to the Church of God.

Just one month earlier, in far-away India the Divine Spirit laid the same burden upon the servants of God, and guided them—without any conscious connection with the prayer-movement in other lands —to form a prayer-circle of those who would unite to plead for the outpoured Spirit upon that dark and needy land. Manifestly the Spirit of God was simultaneously moving the people of God in various parts of the world to pray for the same thing, and creating the cry for that which He was preparing to do.

Later we shall see how the year 1902, when the circles of prayer were formed, stands out as the time when world-wide the praying people of God—— including, we doubt not, many prayer-groups, and praying hearts, not visibly linked with the world wide circles—united in one accord to ask for the promised Pentecost.

It is significant also that in this year of 1902 a pamphlet entitled "A Revival Call to the Churches" was issued, and obtained a wide circulation, and another pamphlet called "Back to Pentecost," issued the same year, showed how God was leading the thoughts of His people, and preparing them for His purposes of grace.

Can we discern any immediate effects of the world-girdling prayer? Within a year there began to be signs of awakening in various quarters, and the "Voice of the Lord" was "upon the waters," but not yet any movement of the Spirit which could be said to bear to the eyes of the world the characteristics of Pentecost.

As in the days of Anna and Simeon, there were many hidden souls in the secret of His counsels. One such was present at Keswick at the time of the call to prayer. She had offered herself to Him some two years before this for the special service of intercession, and the story of His dealings is best told in her own words:-

"I had read words to this effect, 'If even one life could be fully surrendered to God to use as He wanted for prayer, most wonderful results would follow—and He needs such an one.' Then I knelt down, and very humbly told Him if He would take me and use me for prayer, I would be willing. When I said fully from my heart, 'Yes, Lord,' it seemed as if a hand was placed on me pressing me lower and lower, until I had no life left in me—and I wept.

For some months I was used for prayer in small things, but one day about six months later all was utter darkness. As usual I went to Him, but the darkness continued for about a week. Then one morning, about ten o'clock, the agony became terrible, and I cried, 'Lord, what is it?' He answered, 'Come with Me, and I will show you the sin in this place.' We seemed to go into all the worst parts of the district, and I saw sin as never before. I cried out for the people. The prayer was, '0 Lord, send a Revival into this place.' Then came perfect peace until the next morning at the same time, when the Lord called me again, and took me further afield. The same thing happened for a whole week until I was agonizing for a ' World-wide Revival,' as He took me into places where the Gospel had never been heard. Then all this ceased.

From this time I was watching for the Revival, and wondering how the Lord would send it. When we heard of any special one being used, I went to the Lord and said, 'Is this Thine instrument, Lord?' and He answered, ' Only one, child. Again I went about another much-used soul, and the same answer came, with this addition, 'I have something more than this.'

At Keswick in 1902—the first I had ever attended—'Prayer Circles' were announced for a 'World-wide Revival.' Then I went to the Lord and cried, 'Lord, why must they pray for what Thou hast already promised?' Then He said, 'This Revival is an accomplished fact in My Kingdom,' and I said, 'Why does it not come, Lord, without these Prayer Circles? He replied, 'I am ready, but My children are not. Before it comes they must preach the word of the Cross—the message of Calvary.'

"I am ready, but My children are not," shows that the world-wide circles of prayer were mainly necessary for the purpose of creating desire among the people of God, and preparing the channels for the coming "rain." "They must preach the Cross," tells us also that God Himself cannot send "Revival" until the Gospel of Calvary is proclaimed.

But now with one accord the cry has ascended to heaven. The Christ upon His Throne is ready to bless. The blood of the Son of God which has been "trodden under foot," and counted "a common thing," shall be borne witness to from heaven.

Whither shall we now turn our eyes to see His workings. Can we perceive a marked renewal of the preaching of the Cross? Yea, verily. Early in 1903 the records in the papers showed on every side that the messengers of God were being led by Him to proclaim afresh the message of Calvary. At annual meetings, opening services, and special conferences, the key-note again and again was the "Need for direct preaching of the Cross," whilst a well-known religious paper remarked that there were "welcome signs of reversal to the old Gospel of Calvary."

In the light of all this it is significant to find that at the Keswick Convention of 1903, when the windows of heaven were opened, and the Holy Spirit swept as an overflowing stream over the huge gatherings of five thousand men and women—many of them come from distant parts of the earth to seek the power of the Holy Ghost—He unveiled to them in fresh and vivid power the Cross of Calvary, for almost every servant of God entrusted with His messages proclaimed with one accord the "Word of the Cross" as the power of God to save from the bondage as well as the guilt of sin, and "crucified with Christ" as the secret of deliverance was the theme on every hand.*

In 1902 the Holy Ghost had drawn His people to pray for a World-wide Revival, and in 1903 the Eternal Spirit broke forth upon the people of God gathered from the ends of the earth, and leads them back to CAL-VARY.

Moreover, in this same year of 1903, in far-away India the Spirit of God unveiled to one of His honoured servants the Cross of Calvary in new and vivid power, revealing to him that for forty years He had been preparing him for the work of sending forth the "Word of the Cross to every tongue and tribe and nation," in millions of booklets containing the full-orbed message of Calvary.

Yes, truly prayer must prepare God's people for the moving forth of the Spirit in Pentecostal power, and when the Holy Spirit comes forth He bears witness to Calvary, as in the days of the first Pentecost in Jerusalem.

"O! ANFON DI YR YSBRYD GLA N."

Oh! send Thy Holy Spirit, Lord,
In Jesu's blessed name,
Oh ! let Thy Spirit now descend
In tongues of sacred flame!

According to Thy promise, Lord,
Shed freely from above
The Holy Spirit in His strength
To manifest Thy love.

2. The Principality of Wales

The Prophet of the Revival --His Last Message to Wales In 1903--The First Llandrindod Convention in August, 1903

"The sound of abundance of rain." I KINGS xviii. 41.

BUT where in these days can be found the conditions necessary for the mighty working of God? It must be, and can only be, where the Atonement of Christ is proclaimed, and the Scriptures accepted sincerely as the Word of the living God.

We look towards the little Principality of Wales, and find these conditions there. Speaking generally the pulpit has been true to the Evangelical faith in all its essentials, and the gospel of the grace of God has been faithfully preached to the people. The nation has clung, as a whole, to the faith of their fathers—the exception being the few who have been touched by the spirit of criticism and unbelief so prevalent in other lands. True the people may have been living upon the traditions of the past, yet there has not been departure from the "faith once for all delivered to the saints." Wales has also had special advantages in its Sunday schools, where people of all ages gathered to learn the Word of God, and earnest efforts were directed to make the teaching effectual by systematic study and Scripture examinations. Then, again, we find the congregational festivals for singing placing the words of hymns full of the message of Calvary into the people's memories. Groups of churches would practice the same selection of hymns through the winter, and then a day would be set apart for a festival under the conductor-ship of a leading musical teacher. The late Joseph Parry, Mus. Doc., said, in conducting one of these festivals not long before he died, that the coming revival would be a singing one! With the Gospel of Calvary in their minds, and the hymns about Calvary in their memories, the nation needed but the breath of God to quicken their traditional faith into living power.

The All-Wise God looks forth upon the world, and finds here in this little country the conditions necessary for the breaking forth of His Spirit in Pentecostal power.

Let us see whether there are traces of the "prayer movement" in the Principality. We do not know whether the story of the world-girdling prayer circles reached many in Wales, but we find the Holy Spirit creating in individuals, and groups of twos and threes, the very same cry He was calling forth all over the world.

In 1901 the Lord drew near to one of His servants in the ministry, and gave him such a revelation of His glory that he cried, like Isaiah, "Woe is me," and entered on a life in God unknown before. Then, in a quiet spot on the banks of a Welsh river, burdened over the spiritual condition of the country, he spent hours in prayer, pleading with God with many tears that He would come forth in power and work in the land. Again, in a quiet town in the western part of Wales, we hear of two and three women meeting together for prayer during several years, pleading for "Revival" among the women of the town.

We go to the Rhondda Valley, where afterwards the Spirit of God swept with great power, and hear of some who for years had been pleading for a Revival which should "sweep over the whole world." We do not wonder that such souls are taken in to the secrets of God, the Holy Spirit saying to one of them just three days before the valley was moved by the mighty tide of life, " Get thee up . . . there is the sound of abundance of rain."

We find in Monmouthshire the hand of the Lord upon two sisters, one an invalid, who, during 1903-1904, were burdened over the prevalence of sin, and the increase of crime in the county, one sister saying, tearfully, "I cannot sleep day nor night because my dear Lord is despised and set at naught." Another child of God—a retiring, timid lady— bemoaning the deadness of the churches, said, "I shall die unless God exerts His power, and sends a Revival!"

We hear of three ministers of the Gospel meeting together in May, 1903, for prayer and conference, drawn together by a sense of need; utterly dissatisfied with their own Christian experience, and distressed at the condition of their churches, with worldliness and apathy among their officers and members. Once again we see it is a group of three! They decided to form a "prayer circle," and fixed 10 o'clock each morning as the time to pray for each other and their churches. This prayer-group we shall refer to again, but just here it throws light upon the Spirit drawing forth prayer in Wales in unconscious accord with the world-wide circles of prayer. The Spirit of God was manifestly brooding over the land, and doubtless there are many names recorded in heaven of others burdened with a similar consciousness of need, who were drawn out in Spirit-taught prayer, both in the ordinary prayer-meetings of the Churches, and Young People's Socie-ties, as well as alone, with God.

In the momentous year of 1902—the prayer-movement year, we may call it—as we look toward Wales we see also a figure standing out like Moses on Pisgah's mount, beholding the land of far distances. One who has since been called the "prophet of the Revival." The late Dean Howell, of St. David's, or "Llawdden,"—to use his bardic name. A dignitary of the Church of England, like Solomon, he had "largeness of heart even as the sand that is on the sea-shore!" so that he was beloved of all sections of the people as a saintly man of God, a patriot, preacher-orator, and bard.

In the closing month of 1902, in his far-away home on the extreme western point of the Principality, at the age of 83, " Llawdden" looks out upon his beloved land. Conscious of standing on the brink of eternity, with earth-born things fading from his gaze, and the light of heaven shin-ing upon him, he sends out a message to his countrymen, since realised to be wondrously prophetic of the Revival.

The Dean first gave a vivid sketch of the spiritual dearth in the land, and then in powerful language emphasised he only remedy to be a spiri-tual awakening. He appealed to all to "create a circle of implorers" who would cry to God in the words of Isaiah, "Oh, that Thou wouldest rend the heavens, and come down." Then beseeching his readers to consecrate themselves to make a revival the chief end of their desire, he closed with the following memorable words :— "Take notice, if it were known that this was my last message to my fellow-countrymen throughout the length and breadth of Wales before being summoned to judgment, and the light of eternity already breaking over me, and it is this—the chief need of my country, and my dear nation at present is a SPIRITUAL REVIVAL THROUGH A SPECIAL OUTPOURING OF THE HOLY GHOST."

The message was issued in a Welsh Magazine in January, 1903, and caused a deep impression throughout the Principality. It proved indeed to be his last message, for shortly after its issue the aged Dean passed to his heavenly reward.

"A spiritual revival through the outpouring of the Holy Ghost" was just what God was leading His people all over the world to pray for, and even then beginning to send upon the Principality of Wales. But before we watch the rising of the tide we must again return to the "Prayer Circle," Keswick, of 1902.

At Keswick that same year were found two Welsh ministers who told how thirteen Welsh people, gathered in 1896 at the Keswick Convention, met together one afternoon for a prayer meeting for Wales, asking God

Himself to give to Wales a similar Convention for the deepening of the spiritual life. For six years this petition lay before the Lord, until in the seventh year—which in the Scriptures always speaks of God's fulness of time—the Lord's time to answer had come.

Again without using any of the usual "machinery" the Spirit of God immediately began to move toward the arrangement of a Conference for Wales, by a series of steps of such remarkable guidance, and wonderful coincidences, that so far as anything can be said to be wrought of God, with the least touch of human hand, so far can it be said that God Himself arranged, and brought to fruition, the Convention which became one of the channels for the rivers of life to Wales. When in September, 1902, the aged Dean was asked whether, in his judgment, the time was ripe for such a Conference for Wales, he stood, and with his hands raised, and his eyes lifted heavenward, he said, "I am an old man on the edge of eternity, and I say that if such a Conference could take place, God-given and not man-made, it would be an incalculable blessing to Wales."

From this time on, with much prayer and wise counsels, he entered into all the detailed arrangements for the Conference, giving his very last strength and labours to the furthering of what he believed would tend to bring about the "spiritual high tide" which he, at this very time, urged upon his countrymen as " the chief need of Wales."

Meanwhile the Spirit of God was working in the Principality. We have referred to the group of three ministers who banded together for prayer in May, 1903. They were conscious that the first step to blessing for their churches was to get right with God themselves. They agreed to pray daily, but they could not see clearly the way of the better life. In their perplexity they decided to write to a well-known London minister, begging him, if possible, to find time to meet a company of ministers in Glamorganshire to give them spiritual counsel and help. He replied that he could not come just then, but told them of the coming Conference, when he would gladly give them a private interview.

At the very same time—the spring of 1903—in a district in Glamorganshire, four young men, only 18 years of age, were found on a mountain-side holding a prayer-meeting, and pleading with God for a revival in their church, which was in a cold and formal state, converts being few and far between. It transpired that these young men had held their prayer-meeting on the mountain every night for a month past! When this prayer-circle became known, the majority of the church viewed the proceedings with suspicion, and some ignored or mocked the "enthusiasm" of the lads. But they continued to pray on the mountain-side for two whole months, and, to the astonishment of the church, people joined them, and prayed with them, who never visited any place of worship! Some twelve or fourteen were now praying fervently for a revival, until at length the church members were touched, and all became moved with a spirit of prayer and passion for souls. The meetings attended only by four at first now increased to scores, and all testified to the power of God in a special manner.

By this movement among the young people the Pastor himself was drawn to the searching of his own heart and life, asking himself whether he was fully surrendered to Christ, and had received the Holy Ghost. Finally he entered a new plane of spiritual experience and knowledge of the power of God.

There are many other indications of the river of God beginning to rise in the early months of 1903, and unmistakable signs of God working in preparation for some mighty movement of the Spirit. At this crucial point, by the providence of God, came the long-prayed-for Conference, which was held at Llandrindod Wells in August, 1903.

The gatherings were strikingly representative, numbers of clergy and ministers from all parts of the Principality being present, together with some forty of the ministers and evangelists of the "Forward Movement" of the Presbyterian Church of Wales.* So noticeable was the ministerial attendance that a well-known missioner involuntarily remarked, " Wales may be the cradle of the evangelists for the coming Revival!"

There was no set programme for the meetings. The messages of the Lord's messengers bore directly upon the experimental aspect of the Holy Spirit's work in the believer. The putting away of all known sin, deliverance through identification with Christ in His death, and the definite reception of the Holy Ghost as an absolute necessity for all in the service of God, was emphasised, and carried home to hearts by the power of God in such intensity, that on the last two days it was manifest to all that the Spirit of God had come down in the midst.

And what of the group of three who had sought the help of the London minister? One wrote: "Six of us went! [to the Conference.] But the history of that week can never be written—some believed, some doubted, some rebelled! But in a few days each one entered the promised land. We have met once a month ever since, coming from long distances, and we spend a quiet day with God. Our meetings have been indescribable, and we have had a number of Pentecosts."

Many of the ministers and workers returned to their various spheres of labours with new visions and new hopes. As one said, "a new world" had opened to them—and they could not but lead others in! Local conventions began to be held in various places, and the ministers themselves became channels of blessing to their fellow ministers. One Pastor writes that later in 1903, he came in contact with one of these, and saw at once that he had a spiritual experience which he himself had not, but which he had for months been seeking. It was not long before he, too, received the fullness of the Holy Ghost.

3. The Life-Stream at New Quay in February, 1904

The Second Convention at Llandrindod, August, 1904 -- A Midnight Prayer-Meeting -- The Rivers Rising in the Autumn

"Waters issued out from under the threshold." — EZEK. xlvii, I.

ON the Day of Pentecost in Jerusalem the Spirit of God came upon all the company gathered in the upper room, but when the multitude came together it was Peter whom He chose to interpret to the people what had happened, but Peter could not have reaped the three thousand souls without the co-service of the one hundred and nineteen who, with him, had been filled with the Holy Ghost.

It has been said of the Awakening in Wales that it is the "Acts of the Apostles up-to-date." And we cannot but think that this is so, not only in its manifestations, but in the way in which the Pentecost has come upon the land. The movement is Divine and Heaven-born—and so was Pentecost. Yet in Jerusalem the Spirit of God did not come first upon the multitudes, but upon the company in the upper room, and through them into the world in exact fulfilment of the Lord's words, "I will send Him unto you. And He will convict the world." (John xvi. 7, 8).

The law of the Holy Spirit's working has not changed, and we should doubtless find, were we able to see all as known to God, that He has had His "120" in Wales, prepared by Him to be channels for the outflowing Spirit in this great awakening. It is important for the children of God in other countries to realise this, so that they may yield themselves to Him, that through them He may send rivers of life to " all nations" in this day of His power.

Let us look again from the Mount of God, and watch the way that the life-streams began to break out in divers places.

We will turn our eyes first to Cardiganshire, to a little township called New Quay, lying on the fringe of Cardigan Bay, and fifteen miles from a railway station. Here in this out-of-the-way place the Lord had quietly been preparing instruments for the coming Pentecost.

With one of the strange coincidences which makes partnership with the Holy Ghost in service more romantic than any earthly romance, the All-seeing Lord ordained that one of the mightiest rivers should have its rise in the native place, and childhood's church, of one of the ministers who asked of God at Keswick blessing for his native land!

In the momentous year of 1902 a minister in New Quay—whose great grandfather was one of the first band of preachers organised by Howell Harris—had been aroused to spiritual need by the words of a friend from India, and of another who told him he feared he was "backsliding," as he noticed the absence of pathos in his voice when preaching! Aroused to a sense of need for greater blessing in his ministry, he sought this through Bible Study and books on prayer, until at last he entered into a fuller life in reading Dr. Andrew Murray's book, "With Christ in the School of Prayer."

The conviction grew upon him that the Spirit of God alone must save the church and the world. Meeting another minister in November, 1903, they exchanged confidences over the burden on their hearts about the churches, and their need of more abundant life. Neither of these brethren had attended the Llandrindod Conference, but after prayer they determined to recommend to the Presbytery that a Convention for the deepening of the spiritual life be held. The Missioners chosen were three, who received, to use the words of one, "fresh inspiration at Llandrindod." In the choice of these messengers God again showed Himself far above the ways of men. The whole district of South Cardiganshire is essentially Welsh, scarcely more than one English chapel being within a radius of twenty to thirty miles, yet one speaker was a minister who rarely preached in anything but English, the other was one who never preached in Welsh, and the third—the wife of one—a lady who had never spoken in public, excepting once at the " Forward Movement" meetings following the Conference at Liandrindod !

The Convention was for delegates, and there was only one public meeting, but at this meeting, through the words of the handmaid of the Lord, the heart of a young girl was touched, the consequences of which she, or others, little dreamed of at the time.

Meanwhile the Pastor of the church had been moved of God in the same November (1903) to commence a Young People's Meeting in order to counteract the worldly spirit growing among them. One Sunday evening in January, 1904, the pastor preached from the text "This is the victory that overcometh the world." He was strangely drawn out to describe the world as he saw it then depicted before his spiritual vision. To his private house that evening the afore-mentioned young girl wended her way. Shy and retiring, she knew not how to tell him the burden on her soul. She walked up and down outside the house for half-an-hour, and then, gaining courage to enter, said, "Oh, how can I tell you! I cannot live like this. I saw the 'world' in your sermon to-night. I am under its feet. Help me." After some conversation the Pastor found that she thought she was saved, but she was afraid to yield entirely to the Saviour, and own Him as Lord. "He may ask me things difficult," she said, and she would not that night commit herself to the Lordship of Jesus Christ.

On the following Sunday morning, in February, 1904, the Spirit of God bade the Pastor introduce some new feature into the Young People's Meeting held after the morning service, and then it came to him to ask for testimony, definite testimony, as to what the Lord had done for their own souls.

One or two rose to speak, but it was not testimony. It was just then that the same young girl— shy, nervous, intelligent—stood up in tears, and with clasped hands simply said with deep pathos, "Oh, I love Jesus Christ with all my heart." Instantly the Spirit of God appears to have fallen upon the gathering, and all were deluged with tears. It was the beginning of the visible manifestation of the Spirit breaking out in life-streams which afterwards would touch thousands of souls.

As at Pentecost, the blessing was soon noised abroad. Doors began to open on every hand, and the young people, led by their minister, conducted meetings throughout the south of the county, the Lord working with them in manifest power. But as yet the world knew little of what was going on.

In August, 1904, the second Convention at Llandrindod took place, when the testimony meeting revealed how deep a work had been wrought in 1903. A minister, writing to the "Goleuad "—a Welsh paper—said that at the 1904 Conference many saw a door of hope for revival in Wales in the near future." Referring to the testimony meeting he said :—

"It was a luxury to hear ministers and laymen giving expression to the change that had taken place in their ministry and in their own personal lives since the Convention of 1903. Reference was made to a more intense consecration, to habits set aside, to a fuller dependence on the power of the Holy Ghost, and the many souls born in consequence thereof. Some testified that the Bible was a new book to them; others that prayer was easier and more powerful than it used to be . . . . .It is manifest that better days are about to dawn, and blessed are those believers who are willing now to consecrate themselves as worthy mediums for the Holy Ghost in the next revival."

The Spirit of God broke forth again in glorious power that momentous week in 1904, and none will ever forget the closing morning meeting, when overcome by the revelation of the fullness of redemption purchased for the sinner by Jesus Christ our Lord, with hands raised and bowed heads, the audience sang again, and again, and again, "Crown Him Lord of all." Neither will the message that night on '' Exuberance of life in Jesus Christ '' ever be forgotten. Truly God was leading His people into open vision of Himself, and preparing them for the exuberant life which He has since shown in object-lesson before the eyes of the world.

All through 1903 and 1904 the underground currents were quietly deepening and sometimes breaking out to the surface, until the time drew near when the flood-gates opened and the Spirit of God broke out upon the land as a "tidal-wave" sweeping all things before it, or, to use another figure, as a "forest fire" consuming all things it touched.

We have seen the beginning of the life-streams in New Quay in February, 1904. Let us follow to their churches some of the ministers who entered into the Spirit-filled life in August, 1903. They tell of a midnight prayer-meeting at the 1904 Conference, when they all consecrated themselves afresh to God for His use, and definitely asked the Lord to raise up some one to usher in the Revival! A month later two of their churches were in the midst of a mighty awakening, when scores were converted!

One returned to his people, and urged upon them the fullness of the Spirit for every believer. This soon aroused attention, and the subject became talked about by the colliers at work. Some opposed, but some yielded, and several young men surrendered to be possessed by the Holy Ghost. At the end of September prayer-meetings began to be held on every week-night, until the schoolroom was filled, and they had to adjourn to the chapel, where again they gathered every night for three weeks longer. The prayer-meetings were then intermingled with testimony meetings, and afterwards special services were held conducted by one of the ministers who had entered the Spirit-filled life. At these fifty found the Saviour, and large numbers of young people received in actual experience their "Pentecost." By the end of the year one hundred and twenty souls were added to the Lord.

Another minister who entered the Spirit-filled life in 1903 returned to his church fervently praying for an outpouring of the Spirit, and slowly signs began of better things approaching. People in the church who had taken offence with each other were reconciled. Unity prepared the way of the Lord, and then on November 20, 1904, the Spirit of God broke out.

The Pastor had been preaching at a mission station in the morning, but passing the mother-church on his way home, he entered, and found the service still on. Something had occurred! There was not a dry eye in the place! The people were shedding tears and smiling at the same time. One of the elders, in a broken voice, said that they had experienced a most wonderful meeting. The Holy Spirit had come in such mighty power that they decided to dispense with Sunday school and sermons and spend the day in prayer and praise. "Under normal conditions it would be necessary to give due notice of re-arrangements of this kind, and to have them sanctioned by a church meeting," writes the Pastor, " but now the Holy Spirit took possession heeding not our arrangements, and no one had the courage or the desire to protest!" From this time meetings were held every night, and some of the young people became possessed by the Spirit to such a remarkable degree that the "Acts of the Apostles became more intelligible" to all. Many were led into full surrender to Christ as King, and gave soul-stirring testimonies. Those who had hitherto taken but a passive interest in the work of the church sprang forward, and became bold witnesses for Christ. Open-air meetings were organised when even young women raised their voices in testimony, and those who had been too diffident to take part in public service, now did not hesitate to speak even to drunkards coming out of public-houses, and kneel down and pray for them in the open streets.

Another minister returned to his church bearing witness to the Spirit-filled life, and signs of blessing began in September, 1903, as a deep thirst for better things slowly grew among the members. In July, 1904, the Pastor commenced a special meeting after the ordinary evening service, particularly for those who desired to live the Spirit- filled life. The Holy Spirit came upon that meeting in such manifest power that all present were overwhelmed, and remarkable testimonies were afterwards given by many. On a later Sunday evening, the Spirit of God broke forth again in the ordinary service. Strong men were broken down, and said afterwards that they felt as if they must shout to relieve their pent-up feelings. Several young men gave themselves to Christ in this service. Sunday after Sunday the place was filled by the Holy Ghost, and several conversions took place. At the close of one service held in October all who desired to consecrate themselves to the Lord, and go out and seek the lost, were asked to meet in the schoolroom, and here the "Revival" began. Souls were saved night after night for weeks succeeding.

"But," writes the Pastor, "although we had completed ten weeks of prayer meetings, and many souls were gathered in, I still felt the church as a whole had not received her Pentecost. Early in December 1904, in a memorable prayer meeting several crossed the line, and entered the promised land. Some men were so literally filled with the Spirit that others could have said 'They are drunk with new wine.' A great passion for souls took possession of many hearts from this time, and in one week seventy souls were gathered in. Many made public confession of sins, and consecrated themselves to Christ. After 11 o'clock one Saturday night ten men yielded to the Saviour, and over one hundred and fifty confessed Christ ere 1904 closed. The whole movement without doubt had its origin in my own awakening. After I surrendered all conscious sin and yielded entirely to Christ, a new power was immediately felt in my ministry. Now I have a NEW church, with a large number of men and women who have been filled with the Holy Spirit, and are used to win souls."

BOOK 2

The Religous Revival in Wales 1904

by Awstin and other special correspondents of the Western Mail, London, 1905

Preface

Preface by "Eilir": Past and Present Revivals in Wales

The daily press in Wales during the present revival is passing through a new and strange experience. For the first time in its history its columns are devoted to reporting the proceedings in connection with any movement of the kind. Considering that it is a novice in this kind of work, it must be admitted that it performs its task by no means an easy one tolerably successfully. In the estimation of some critics, indeed, so successfully does it do its work that the present awakening has been called, somewhat irreverently, "a newspaper revival." The press, it is true, has been the means of making it known, but the revival itself spreads by its own inherent force and would have covered the land independently of any encouragement from the daily or weekly newspaper.

It was a small fire that burnt at Loughor when the "Western Mail" gave its first account of the revival, but it required no seer to perceive that in that bright flame were all the possibilities of a huge conflagration that would sooner or later affect the whole country The Loughor movement bore all the marks of a genuine and spontaneous revival, as anybody who tested it by the light of past awakenings in Wales might have seen. Such upheavals invariably spring from small beginnings, so small that for weeks; and some months, they fail to arrest public attention.

The Welsh people have always been easily acted upon by religious influences. This is characteristic of the emotional Celtic race. In ancient and medieval Wales the people were often roused from spiritual sleep, now by a missionary saint, and again by some fiery preaching friar. The history of the pre-Reformation Church contains several notable instances of religious emotionalism. In the seventeenth century pulpit power was greatly in evidence in some parts of Wales.

One or two instances must suffice. The famous Vicar Prichard by his preaching attracted immense congregations everywhere, and made a deep impression upon the people. Revivals on many occasions broke out under the moving eloquence of Griffith Jones, of Llanddowror. Jones, in fact, was the precursor of the greatest revival Wales has ever experienced, that of 1755, of which the preaching of Howel Harris, of Treveeca, was the immediate cause. Almost simultaneously, however, with the Breconshire movement occurred that of Llangeitho. A notable fact in connection with both is that they originated in church. Harris felt himself endued with power from on high after partaking of the Holy Communion in Talgarth Church on Easter day, 1735, and Rowlands, whilst in the act of reading the Litany at Llangeitho Church, brought down the Divine spark which eventually grew into a consuming fire. In a few years'time no fewer than ten ordained clergymen (Harris himself was a layman) were engaged in the work of preaching the Gospel in all sorts of places, both consecrated and unconsecrated, and of spreading the revival in Wales. Ecclesiastical authority interposed, but to no purpose. It was only a fighting against stronger odds.

The movement grew and developed despite all obstacles, until at length it touched Wales at all points. We are now able to realise that it was destined to change the whole course of Welsh history. Though, however, it began in church, it was carried on outside its pale, with disastrous results to the 'Old Mother.' We who live in these far-off days can form no adequate conception of the mighty influences that operated in those days in religious circles in Wales and the marvellous results which followed. The face of the whole country, morally speaking, was changed. A new and powerful denomination sprang up, and new life was breathed into those religious bodies which had previously existed, one only excepted the National Church itself.

During the latter half of the eighteenth century several revivals were witnessed, but they were all more or less local. Seven revivals, it is said, broke out in Harris's time at Liangeitho alone. The most notable of the awakenings was that which occurred during the last decade of the century (1791-2). It is difficult to form a correct estimate of its scope or its results, but we know that it was a very powerful upheaval, and produced marked effects upon young people of both sexes, thousands of whom abandoned their sports and amusements for religious exercises and the bidding and the shebeen for the chapel and the Sunday School.

North Wales was visited by a religious conin 1839, and again the following year, and South Wales witnessed exciting scenes in 1841, 1842 and 1843. The late Dr. Tom Rees, of Swansea, in a letter to the "Christian Witness," in 1843, states that the motive power in the revival of that year was the perusal of a Welsh version of Finney's "Lectures," issued by Mr. E. Griffiths, of Swansea. The effects produced, however, seem to have been transient. for Dr Rees states that the period from the end of 1843 so the summer of 1849 "was a season of almost universal declension."

At the latter date another awakening was experienced in Glamorgan and Monmouthshire, and also in parts of Brecknockshire and Carmarthenshire. It is stated that the terrible visitation of cholera was principly the means of arousing peoples attention in 1849. Fear seems to have had a most rating effect upon peoples minds, for conversions on that occasion were not accompanied by loud cries or promiscuous singing or jumping as had been the case in some former revivals.

We have no record of the number of conversions made on that occasion; but Dr Rees gives a list of Congregational churches with the number of new members added. At Brynmawr there was an increase of 409, Beaufort 396, Alltwen and Pantteg 400, Neath 460, Aberand Carnarvon 650, Tredegar 250, and at Merthyr from 1,200 to 1,500. Other denominations doubt, counted similar gains. A great feature of the revival was the great number of converts 'who pressed together at the same time to the meetings. At Dowlais 240 were given the right hand of fellowship the same Sunday, and at Beaufort 200.

We now come to the greatest shaking of the heavens and the earth the last century knew that of 1859. Its pioneer was Humphrey Jones, a Wesleyan returned from the States, where a powerful awakening had broken out. Jones commenced his campaign at Treiddol, and his preaching soon attracted great attention. In due time Cardiganshire was deeply aroused, and eventually the adjoining counties and the whole of Wales felt the strange new power that was at work. The leading features of the revival were spontaneous prayer meetings among the masses, spirit of union among all religious bodies, and zeal for the conversion of the irreligious. The meetings almost everywhere were conducted just as "the Spirit moved without programme or method and without leader. Anybody prayed or gave out a hymn, and meetings generally terminated owing to the sheer physical exhaustion of the revivalists In hundreds of places people were carried out of chapel unable to move hand or foot. Of an evening the revivalists would, perhaps, go the round of all the chapels in a town or a neighbourhood, and meetings often continued until daybreak. Open-air prayer meetings were frequently held, and ordinary men and women were endowed with a remarkable "gift of tongue," and were unaccountably eloquent. Physical manifestations of feeling were very marked and people often became delirious, giving vent to their emotions by jumping and shouting "Hosannah," "Hallelujah," and such exclamations.

It is estimated that 100,000 new members about a tenth of the population of Wales at the time joined the several religious bodies. One important result of the movement was the improvement produced in the morals of the people. The cause of temperance and social purity was given a powerful stimulus; in fact, the social and religious life of Wales was altogether lifted on to a higher plane.

The 1859 revival also marks a new era in the history of Welsh sacred music. That date saw a revival quite as much in congregational singing as in religion. It was the year in which that landmark in Welsh singing appeared "Ieuan Gwyllts" tune-book. The introduction of the tonic sol-fa system, also, is co-incident with that year, and it was now the singing festival began properly to be the great power we know it in Welsh religious circles to-day. During the past fifty years music has become of paramount importance in Welsh churches and chapels, and sacred song has been powerfully stimulated from outside by the eisteddfod and the concert. No wonder a master of song once observed that "the next revival in Wales would be a singing revival." The remark was founded upon knowledge of the national character and experience of the past half-century. Events around us to-day establish its correctness, and the following pages would serve to illustrate its force.

Chapter 1 - Welsh Religious Revival, 1904

The first public reference to the 1904 revival in Wales was made in the following paragraphs which appeared in the "Western Mail" on November 10.

A WONDERFUL PREACHER.

GREAT CROWDS OF PEOPLE DRAWN TO LOUGHOR.

CONGREGATION STAY TILL HALFPAST TWO IN THE MORN- ING.

A remarkable religious revival is now taking place at Loughor. For some days a young man named Evan Roberts, a native of Loughor, but at present a student at Newcastle-Emlyn, has been causing great surprise by his extraordinary orations at Moriah Chapel, that place of worship having been besieged by dense crowds of people unable to obtain admission. Such excitement has prevailed that the road in which the chapel is situated has been lined with people from end to end.

Roberts, who speaks In Welsh, opens his disby saying he does not know what he (will be led) to say, but that when he is in complete harmony with the Holy Spirit the Holy Spirit (will lead) and he will be simply the medium of His wisdom. The preacher soon after launches out into a fervent and at times imoration. His statements have most stirring effects upon his listeners, many who have disbelieved Christianity for years again returning to the fold of their younger days. One night so great was the enthusiasm invoked by the young revivalist that after a sermon lasting two hours the vast congregation remained praying and singing until half-past two o'clock next morning. Shopkeepers are closing earlier in order to get a place in the chapel, and tin and steel workers throng the place in their working clothes. The only theme of conversation among all classes and sects is "Evan Roberts." Even the taprooms of the public-houses are given over to discussion on the origin of the powers possessed by him. Although barely in his majority, Roberts is enabled to attract the people for many miles around.

He is a Methodist, but the present move is participated in by ministers of all the Nonconformist denominations in the locality. Brynteg Chapel, Gorseinon, is to be the next scene of his ministrations.

This remarkable message indicated such an unusual state of religious fervour that the 'Western Mail' despatched a special correspondent to Loughor to make inquiries, and his vivid report showed that the long-expected revival had really arrived. The special correspondents will now tell their own stories.

Chapter 2 - The Scenes at Laughor

LLANELLY, Friday, November 11.

The ancient township of Loughor, near Llanelly, is just now in the throes of a truly remarkable "revival," the influence of which is spreading to the surrounding districts. Meetings are being held every night attended by dense crowds, and each of them is continued well into the early hours of the next, morning. The missioner is Mr. Evan Roberts, a young man who for some years worked at the Broadoak Colliery. He has spent the whole of his life in the place, and was always known as a man with strong leanings towards religion. He is now preparing for the ministry at a preparatory school at Newcastle-Emlyn. Whatever the source of his power may be, there can be no mistaking the fact that he has moved the whole community by his remarkable utterances, and scores of people who have never been known to attend any place of worship are now making public profession of their conversion. During my visit to Loughor I found that the "revival" was on everyone's tongue, Colliers and tin-platers, shopkeepers and merchants in fact, all classes of the community are to be found among the auditors of this fervid young enthusiast, who declares that the message which he brings to the people is that which is revealed to him by the Holy Spirit. At the close of the remarkable service which is described below I had a short interview with Mr. Roberts. This was at the unearthly hour of 4.30 a.m., after I had gone through a unique seven hours' experience. In answer to my questions Mr. Roberts said that the only explanation of what was now taking place in Loughor was that the Spirit of God was working among the people. Recently death in a very terrible form has come home to the people of Loughor in the wrecking of the express train, and I inquired of Mr. Roberts whether that might account for their readiness to receive the message. He did not, however, think that was at all likely. Asked as to whether he intended devoting himself exclusively to mission work in the future, Mr. Roberts said that in that matter he was in the hands of God.

The meeting at Brynteg Congregational Chapel on Thursday night was attended by those remarkable scenes which have made previous meetings memorable in the life history of so many of the inhabitants of the district. The proceedings commenced at seven o'clock, and they lasted without a break until 4.30 o'clock this (Friday) morning. During the whole of this tune the congregation were under the influence of deep religious fervour and exaltation. There were about 400 people present when I took my seat in the chapel, about nine o'clock. The majority of the congregation were females, ranging from young misses of twelve to matrons with babies in their arms. Mr. Roberts is a young man of rather striking appearance. He is tall and distinguished-looking, with an intellectual air about his clean-shaven face. His eyes are piercing in their brightness, and the pallor of His countenance seemed to suggest that these nightly vigils are telling upon him. There was, however, no suggestion of fatigue in his conduct of the meeting. There is nothing theatrical about his preaching. He does not seek to terrify his hearers; and eternal, torment finds no place in his theology. Rather does he reason with the people and show them by persuasion a more excellent way. I had not been many minutes in the building before I felt that this was no ordinary, gathering. Instead of the set order of proceedings to which we are accustomed at the orthodox religious service, everything here was left to the spontaneous impulse of the moment. The preacher, too, did not remain in his usual seat. For the most part he walked up and down the aisles, open Bible in hand, exhorting one, encouraging another, and kneeling with a third to implore a blessfrom the Throne of Grace.

A young woman rose to give out a hymn, which was sung with deep earnestness. While it was being sung several people dropped down in their seats as if they had been struck, and commenced crying for pardon. Then from another part of the chapel could be heard the resonant voice of a young man reading a portion of Scripture. While this was in progress from the gallery came an impassioned prayer from a woman crying aloud that she had repented of her ways, and was determined to live a better life henceforward. All this time Mr. Roberts went in and out among the congregation offering kindly words of advice to kneeling penitents. He would ask them if they believed, the reply, in one instance being, 'No, I would like to believe, but I can't. Pray for me.' Then the preacher would ask the audience to join him in the following prayer, "Anfon yr Yspryd yn awr, er mwyn Jesu Grist, Amen" \("Send the Holy Spirit now, for Jesus Christ's sake, Amen.") This prayer would be repeated about a dozen times by all present, when the would-be convert would suddenly, rise and declare with triumph, "Thank God, I have now received salvation. Never again will I walk in the way of sinners." This declaration would create a new excitement, and the congregation would joyously sing:

Diolch, iddo, diolch iddo,
Byth am gofio llwch y llawr.

I suppose this occurred scores of times during the nine hours over which the meeting was protracted. A very pathetic feature of the proceedings was the anxiety of many, present for the spiritual welfare of members of their families. One woman was heartbroken for her husband, "who was given to drink." She implored the prayers of the conin his behalf. The story told by, another young woman drew tears to all eyes. She said that her mother was dead, and that her father had given way to sin, so that, she was indeed orphaned in the world. She had attended the meetings without feeling her position, but on the previous day, while following her domestic duties, the Spirit had come upon her, bidding her to speak. And she did speak!her address being remarkable for one who had never spoken before in public. Yet another woman made public confession that she had come to the meeting in a spirit of idle curiosity, but that the influence of the Holy Ghost worked within her, causing her to go down on her knees in penitence. It was now long past midnight, but still there was no abatement in the fervour of the gathering. Fresh fuel was added to the religious fire by Mr. Roberts, who described what had appeared to him as a vision. He said that when he was before the Throne of Grace he saw appearing before him a key. He did not understand the meaning of this sign. Just then, however, three members of the congregation rose to their feet and said that they had been converted. "My vision is-explained," said Mr. Roberts, ecstatically; "it was the key by which God. opened your hearts."

One of the most remarkable utterances of this remarkable night was that of a woman who gave a vivid description of a vision which she had seen on the previous evening. "I saw," she said, "a great expanse of beautiful land, with friendly faces peopling it. Between me and this golden country was a shining river, crossed by a plank. I was anxious to cross, but feared that the plank would not support me. But at that moment I gave myself to God, and there, came over me a great wave of faith, and I crossed I safely."

At 2.30 o'clock I took a rough note of what was then proceeding. In the gallery a woman was praying, and she fainted. Water was offered her, but she refused this, saying that the only thing she wanted was God's forgiveness. A well-known resident then rose and said that salvation had come to him. Immediately following a thanksgiving hymn was sung, while an English prayer from a new convert broke in upon the singing. The whole congregation then fell upon their knees, prayers ascending from every part of the edifice, while Mr. Roberts gave way to tears at the sight. This state of fervency lasted for about ten minutes. It was followed by an even more impressive five minutes of silence, broken only by the sobs of strong men. A hymn was then started by a woman with a beautiful soprano voice. Finally, Mr. Roberts announced the holding of future meetings, and at 4.25 o'clock the gathering dispersed. But even at this hour the people did not make their way home. When I left to walk back to Llanelly I left dozens of them about the road still discussing what is now the chief subject in their lives. They had come prepared with lamps and lanterns, the lights of which in the early hours of darkness were weird and picturesque. In the course of a conversation with our representative on Friday afternoon Mr. Roberts said that he believed we were on the eve of one of the greatest revivals that Wales had ever seen. All the signs of this were present. It was time for us to get out of the groove in which we had walked for so long. He himself was converted twelve or thirteen years ago, and ever since then he had been praying for the Holy Ghost to come upon him. That it had come he was certain. It was one thing for a man to be converted and quite another to receive the baptism of the Spirit. The meetings they had had were glorious experiences. When they opened a meeting they had no idea when it would conclude. Only one thing could be said, and that was that it would not conclude until some definite point had been gained.

Asked how many converts had been made, Mr. Roberts said that he did not call it connor did he believe in the counting of heads. Some people had said that he was doing goodwork. It was not his, however. He was simply an instrument in the hand of God, and he wanted men to receive the joy of religion,, as he had found it. Our fathers had their religion, and too often it made them gloomy. In those cases the "joy" of religion had not been experienced.

The revival originated in the Calvinistic Methodist Church, New Quay. The "fire" broke out on the morning of the second Sunday in February last, in a crowded Christian Endeavour meeting, after the morning service, when a young lady, moved by the words and appeal of a lay speaker, arose in the midst of the congregation, and in a clear voice, intense and pathetic, I love Jesus with all my heart." Her soul seemed to be in every word. Unaccountable power accompanied her simple testimony, and seemed to overwhelm the people. After this the meetings multiplied, and some were held in private houses, wherever entrance could be got. In

all the neighbouring villages and towns people were everywhere electri-
fied by the intense passion of the meeting.

This remarkable message indicated such an unusual state of religious
fervour that the 'Western Mail' despatched a special correspondent to
Loughor to make inquiries, and his vivid reportshowed that the long-
expected revival had really arrived. The special correspondents will now
tell their own stories.

Chapter 3 - The Revival Spreads

LOUGHOR, Sunday, November 13th.

The publication given to the, great "revival" in progress at Loughor and the surrounding district has been the means of attracting thousands of people to the various chapels at which these remarkable gatherings are held. I described the meeting held on Thursday night, which did not conclude till close upon five, o'clock on Friday morn. Friday's meeting, was equally protracted,while the meeting on Saturday night even exceeded this length, the lights in the chapel not being extinguished until after five o'clock.

All the gatherings were alike in that they were marked by the same ecstatic fervour, as distinguished the meeting already described. By this time Mr. Evan Roberts who is the guiding spirit of this wonderful mission, has come to dispense with the address with which, in the earlier days of the movement, he commenced each gathering. His impassioned oratory has done its work, and now the conduct of the proceedings is left almost altogether in the hands of the congregation. How thoroughly they enter into it may be gauged by the length to which each, meeting is carried on.

As might have been expected, some extraordinary incidences are taking place each day outside the chapel walls. On Friday afternoon, for instance, a young man engaged on a farm in the vicinity was sent by his master with a cartload of turnips to Loughor. Earlier in the week he had come under the spell of the missioner, and might be described as one of his converts. When nearing Loughor he was approached by a woman in deep distress, who, with tears in her eyes, besought him to come and pray for her husband. Like the disciples of old, he forthwith "left all," and followed the woman to her house. Over an hour elapsed when his employer came to town, and found his horse and cart in charge of two young children. He was directed to the house, and the scene that presented itself there so affected him that he remained to join his prayers with those of the woman and his servant.

During the whole of Saturday prayer meetings were held in various houses, these being continued up to the time of the evening meeting at

Moriah Chapel. On Saturday afternoon two young women who are prominently identified with the revival, went on a preaching mission to Gorseinon. They were joined by other enthusiasts, and they preached and sang
outside several public-houses. Crowds quickly gathered. Here again there
were heard heart-broken outbursts of contrition among the listeners men
and women so like children.

But, perhaps, the most remarkable service of the day was that held in
the middle of a, large gipsy encampment on Kingsbridge Common. The
dwellers in tents received the missioners with a degree of suspicion, which
augured ill for the success of the service. Before the meeting hadbeen long
in progress, however, this suspicion gave way to wonderment, and later on
to devout awe. Then came paroxysms of grief from the female members
of the encampment, some of them tearing their hair in their self-denun.
When the meeting came to a close a collection was made on behalf of the
poor gipsies, and a promise was given them that another service would be
held on Sunday afternoon.

On Saturday night Moriah Chapel was besieged by a tremendous
crowd anxious to obtain admission. Hundreds of people had some from
Llanelly, Swansea, Gowerton, Gorseinon, and other places, and after the
chapel had been filled to its utmost capacity there was yet a surging mass
of people in the roadway. Mr Roberts, seeing this, ordered the old chapel
which is close by to be opened, and services were then simultaneously
held in the two buildings. The scenes that I described on Saturday were re-
enacted at these two meetings. On all hands it could be seen that the people had been moved to their very heart core. What could not fail to impress even the most callous was the impassioned eloquence of men and
women who up to this juncture in their lives had never uttered a word in
public. Is was thrilling to see young colliers uneducated, ignorant, if you
likerise from their pews and speak as if inspired. Mr. Roberts was joined
on this occasion by a fellow-student. Mr. Evans roused his hearers to new
enthusiasm with his account of the revival in Cardiganshire.

Mr. Evans described his visit to Cardigan Fair, and how the crowd at
first refused to hear the message, preferring to go on with their business.
By- and-bye, however, the people gathered around, and they had a most
successful meeting.

The high-water mark of fervour was reached at the meeting in the old
chapel, where, after a young woman had asked the audience to pray for
her brother, a man rose in the gallery and, speaking with passionate eloquence, described the vision which appeared to him on the previous evening. He said that he was alone in his bedroom, when he suddenly felt

that, he was not alone. At the same time a voice seemed to be calling upon him to pray, but he could not pray. This command was thrice repeated, and he fell on his knees, but not a word escaped him. Then, however, the voice bade him to "Throw out the life-line!" Upon this the entire audience rose as by some common instinct and sang as it has been rarely sung before the well-known hymn of which those words are the refrain.

The experience of a young man engaged as a clerk in a Llanelly office is worthy of notice. Like many others, his curiosity was attracted by these meetings, and he determined to be present on Saturday evening. "By reason of the throng" it was nearly three hours before he gained admittance. Seated next to him was a man whose prayer so affected him that he implored the prayers of the congregation in his own behalf, and later on he rose and spoke as a newly-made convert.

Chapter 4 - Meetings and Trecyn

Trecyon, Monday, November 14.

Modest almost to the point of despair was the beginning made by the Evan Roberts revival mission at Trecynon this evening, and the omens pointed to orthodox quietness rather than to a repetition of the exuberance of emotional fervour which has characterised in such a remarkable degree the revival services at Loughor. When the service was timed to commence at Ebenezer Chapel the empty pews were more numerous than the people assembled, and there was a coldness in the atmosphere which boded ill for a successful meeting. Those who know Trea little village which nestles closely on the borders of Aberdare with its trade of religious zeal, will be most surprised to know that Ebenezer was not besieged on such an occasion, and, perhaps, at the same time, they will best appreciate the laconic remark of a village stoic that "the fair at Aberdare was a powerful counter-attraction."

Instead of finding an eager throng outside the gates of the chapel I was surprised to see only some half-dozen small groups of miners and their wives and sons gathered together, just as is their wont on the occasion of the ordinary weekly prayer meeting. Later in the evening the reason for this sparse attendance became obvious. The service commenced so early that workmen had not been given sufficient time to go to their homes from their work and to change their working clothes for those which they considered to be better befitting a religious service. While the few who had seated themselves in the chapel were waiting for the arrival of the young revivalist an elderly man sitting beneath the gallery offered up a prayer, and a young man who was sitting in another part of the building recited the words of the popular Welsh hymn, "Disgwyl 'rwyf ar hyd yr hirnos," the last two lines of which were being repeated when the five young ladies from Loughor who have played so prominent a part in the mission with their speech and song walked up the aisle and seated themselves in the "set fawr." One of them, possessing a sweet mezzo-soprano voice of singular tenderness, sang Happy Day," and the early coldness was already beginning to thaw under the influence of the intensifying fervour with which the refrain was sung and sung again. The melody was in full swing when Mr. Roberts took his seat beneath the pulpit. Before uttering a word he approached the old man who had been the first to pray, and grasped his hand. The building by this time was filling rapidly. Evan Roberts looked pale, but was full of animation. While another hymn was being sung he walked up and down the aisle, swinging his arms and clapping his hands. At times lie gave a, short, sharp spring off his right foot, and smiled joyously upon the people around him. There was no conventionality, no artificiality or affectation in his manner. The expression on his open, attenuated, and distinctly intellectual face was that of a man with a mission, and reminded one of the portraits to be seen in so many Welsh homesteads of men who were leaders in the two previous religious revivals in Wales.

Speaking in Welsh, He discarded the stereotyped preface so commonly in vogue among preachers in the Principality, and straightway declared the faith that was in him. He had not come there, he said, to frighten them with a discourse on the terrors of everlasting punishment. His belief was that the love of Christ was a powerful enough magnet to draw the people. That was his own personal experience, and he had found a joy which was far beyond human expression. No one but the true believer knew in reality what it was to have a light heart and unalloyed happiness. Denominationalism did not enter into his religion. Some people had said he was a Methodist. He did not know what he was. Sectarianism melted in the fire of the Holy Spirit, and all men who believed became one happy family. For years he was a faithful member of the Church, a zealous worker, and a free giver. But he had recently discovered that he was not a Christian, and there were thousands like him. It was only since he had made that discovery that a new light had come into his life. That same light was shining upon all men if they would but open their eyes and their hearts. Reverting to sectarianism, he said that whilst sect was fighting against sect the devil was clapping his hands with glee and encouraging the fight. Let all people be one, with one object the salvation of sinners. Men refused to accept the Gospel and confess because, they said, of the gloom and uncertainty of the future. They looked to the future without having opened their eyes to the infinite glories of the present. They talked about the revival of 1859. Why, there would be a perpetual revival if men would only keep their hearts open instead of closing them to every influence. If anyone had come there that evening with the intention of making an impression, he advised him or her to refrain. Unless they felt that they were moved to speech or song, let them keep their peace. He did not come there to glorify himself. Glad tidings had come from Loughor concerning a mission among the gipsies in their encampment near that place. The soul of a gipsy was of no less value than that of any other human creature.

Such was the substance of Mr. Roberts's address. He spoke for an hour and a quarter under evident restraint, and in a quiet, confident style. He made no attempt at rhetoric, and was never at a loss for a phrase or a word. Those who might have come to scoff and did not remain to pray must, at any rate, have been deeply impressed with the profound earnestness of the young man, and there is no doubting his absolute sincerity and conviction.

Immediately he had resumed his seat two elderly women rose simultaneously, one speaking in Welsh and the other in English. The voice of her who spoke the latter language rang out clearly, and a common thrill trembled through the assembly as a. breath of wind runs across the sea. Her last words were, I love my Master because I know what He has done for me," and then she fell back in the pew. A young woman came forward with the Bible in her hand and was preparing to read, when Mr. Roberts asked the people to sing "Duw mawr y maith," the stirring words of which were repeated several times. After reading a portion of Scripture the young woman knelt down in prayer, and an impassioned fervour spread into all parts of the crowded chapel.

During the remainder of the night many men and women broke forth in prayer and song, and a meeting which had opened so coldly was in a white heat of religious enthusiasm before the last word had been said.

Chapter 5 - Full Day of Noble Work

TRECYNON, Tuesday, November 15th.

The indications of the spread of a religious revival in Wales are increasing in force as well as spreading over a larger area, and the fact that the movement is not due to the overpowering fervour and eloquence of any great preacher or preachers only proves that the country seems to be ripening for manifestations of the "hwyl" in a rising tide which thousands are apparently waiting, watching, and praying for. The gatherings at Trecynon, Aberdare, conducted by Mr. Evan Roberts, of Loughor, and the five young singing evangelists who accompany him are attracting crowds, not only from the immediate neighbourhood, but mixed companies of the sceptic, the doubtful, the curious, the zealous, the enthusiastic, and the stern believer in the advent of the revival from distant towns and villages; and when the silver-tongued orators of Welsh pulpit and pew shall have caught the infectious spirit of these pioneers of the movement there can, in the present state of expectancy, only be one result an upheaval of religious forces which will undoubtedly electrify the Principality.

Ebenezer Chapel, where today's proceed were conducted by Mr. Evan Roberts, is the Welsh Congregational Chapel so famous in connection with what was known as Edwards Morgan's revival in 1859, and although Aberdare does not appear, as yet, to have particularly joined Trecynon, there can be no doubt that before the week is out similar services will be held there.

Perhaps the greatest mystery of the whole movement at present is that the central figure of the revival, Mr. Evan Roberts, is not gifted with the remarkable eloquence which is generally the attribute of a man who sways multitudes. As I heard a man remark, wonderingly, "We have plenty of better speakers, and, possibly, abler men, but they do not seem to be imbued with the same power as he wields in drawing these immense crowds and keeping them together. At present I can only account for it by the fact that he comes from the midst of the Loughor fire."

That is just it. He neither preaches nor harangues; he simply talks, pleads, exhorts, explains; tells his own story simply and winningly, and smilingly invites. He does not even give out the electrifying Welsh hymns with the effect which many can impart to the stirring words; but he is evidently sincere, and he prays with the fervour of a man whose heart is deeply moved. The young ladies who accompany him are not professional singers; but they are manifestly touched with the spirit of singing pilgrims, and, in summing up the strangeness of the power thus introduced, one can only be reminded of the story of the humble origin of the disciples of old, as "the fishermen of the Sea of Galilee." But the spontaneous striking up of a hymn or the starting of an address in Welsh or English, or the uttering of a devout prayer by men or women in the congregation, in the body of the chapel, or the gallery, from pulpit, big pew, or anywhere that may be occupied by the person who rises, naturally tends to infuse enthusiasm and decentralise the work.

The prayer meeting held at Ebenezer this morning is described as a wonderful one, lasting from ten o'clock until 1.15. Men had remained home from work in order to attend it. People who had come long distances the previous day had remained in the village overnight in order to join.

"Who conducted it?" I asked. "No one," was the reply; "but Evan Roberts prayed." The "Holy Spirit led." declared Evan Roberts himself.

At the night meeting, announced for seven o'clock, there, was a full chapel before the time fixed, and Evan Roberts, now and then rising and pacing the "set fawr," seemed agitated with expectancy. He got up at five minutes to seven and gave out a hymn of the Church Militant "Mae'r Iesu'n myn'd I ryfel," and, after it had been sung, took the words for the text of an address lasting nearly half an hour. Then he invited the congregation to sing:

"Marchog Iesu yn llwyddianus, Gwisg dy gleddyf ar dy glun."

and the tide of feeling seemed to rise gradually as the meeting proceeded. One of the young ladies in the big seat started singing:

"O happy day that fixed my choice, On Thee, my Saviour and my God,"

And the congregation joined heartily in the refrain, which was repeated again and again. The singer stopped, and stated that she had that day visited some gipsies, and that two of them had accompanied her to that meeting. It was a happy day for her, and she could not help singing "Happy day, happy day, when Jesus washed my sins away," and she commenced singing again, and the "repeats" were more fervent than before, indicating clearly the influence of the words and the music, as well as the feeling, upon the congregation.

A man in the gallery afterwards prayed. Mr. Roberts then delivered a brief address. He remarked that it was not for ministers or deacons to do the work of the Churches alone, but for all to work together, and then the revival of which they were now only opening the gates would come. Would any "backslider" get up and re-join the Lord's Church? They need not be afraid of the term "backslider." Coming back was the great thing. Promptly came the response, A man rose in the congregation, and spoke a, few words in a low voice, and spontaneously the crowded congregation sang:

"Gwaed y Groes sy'n codi fyny, 'Reiddil yn goncwerwyr mawr; Gwaed y Groes sydd yn darostwng Cewri cedyrn fyrdd i lawr. Diolch iddo, Byth am goflo llwch y llawr."

Without repeating the full verses, the now thoroughly roused congregation sang the refrain of the next verse:

"Pen Calfaria, Nac aed hwnw byth o'm cof."

An old lady rose in the body of the chapel and delivered an impassioned Welsh appeal to all to join the people who could sing "0 happy day," and a man seemingly a worker at the lower end of the chapel, gave out, voluntarily, the hymn, "Ni fuasai genyf obaith," which led to fervent singing of the well-known "repeat":

"O rhyw anfeidrol gariad I gofio am danaf fi,"

the eloquent words and music with which the late Gabriel Williams, of Treherbert, thrilled the vast audience in St. James's Hall, London, on a memorable occasion. some years ago. By this time the pulpit, or, rather, rostrum, of the chapel was filled, as well as the pews, and while the conductor of the meeting was walking about quietly, now in the gallery, now in the aisles, four local ministers sat in the rostrum, thoroughly enjoying the service and joining heartily in the singing.

Presently there was a moment's silence, and a North Walian rose and shouted, "Thank God for Llwynffortun, the only man who in days gone by took an interest in the gipsies," and then proceeded to speak at some length, raising and lowering his voice in the cadences of the Welsh

"hwyl," as the old lady already referred to had done. 'While he was proceeding a girl's sweet voice rang out with the words and music of "Gwaed
y groes sy'n codi fyny," and the congregation joined magnificently.

Into the "big seat," and, at the earnest invitation of others, on to the
rostrum went a clerical-looking gentleman the Rev. T. 0. Thomas, formerly schoolmaster of Bedlinog who, without announcing, or being announced, read a portion of Scripture, and fired his hearers by declaring
that he had just come from Loughor, where he had been "in the midst of
the fire." He had spent Sunday there, and could testify to that which was
being done. He was, he said, keenly interested in it. He remembered an
old woman praying for this revival before this young man (pointing to Mr.
Evan Roberts) was born in the words (which he sang)

"O anfon Di yr Ysbryd Glan, Yn enw Iesu mawr, A'i weithrediadau
megys tan, O anfon Ef i lawr"

Needless to say, the touch of the "fire" kindled a kindred fire in the
congregation, and the service was still further strengthened when Mr.
Roberts once more declared that the revival was coming that they were
only "opening the gates," and he asked them to sing:

"Duw mawr y rhyfeddodau maith."

He interspersed maxims and exhortations, even in giving out the
hymn, and then came the deep roll of the resounding bass on the lines:

"Ond Dwyfol ras, niwy rhyfedd yw Na'th holl weithredoedd o bob
rhyw," &c.

Thus were the proceedings continued until a late hour.

Chapter 6 - Crowds at Pontycymmer

PONTYCYMMER, Wednesday, November 16.

Pontycymmer has never witnessed such scenes as those which made a huge throng tremble with a strange excitement at the Congregational Chapel to-night. In response to an invitation from the religious bodies of the town of Pontycymmer, Mr. Evan Roberts came down to the colliery village from Aberdare, and in his simple and unostentatious way created a convulsion of feeling which must have convinced the most sceptical that the revival in Wales is sweeping over Pontycymmer with telling force. People had come from all parts of the Garw Valley to hear this young man, whose fame has spread on every hand, and whose name is already on every tongue. He is spoken of now as the John Wesley of Wales, a man whose message is peace and goodwill. His gospel has no terrors for anyone. There is no gloom in it. His countenance reflects happiness, even to joyousness, and this he imparts to all who listen to him and believes in what ho preaches.

His address at Pontycymmer was similar in tone to that delivered at Trecynon on Monday evening. No attempt was made to set a flame to people's passion with the torch of rhetoric. Evan Roberts's methods are in keeping with his character. He is plain and simple in the severest degree, and his own constant endeavour is to sink his own personality in the depths of his subject.

Those who heard him tonight for the first time were so full of curiosity to know what manner of man he was that their minds for a time were solely intent upon a close and keen observation of his style and mannerisms rather than upon listening to what he had to say. They had read in the "Western Mail" of his habit of swaying his arms and walking along the aisles. He varied not these little idiosyncrasies in the conduct of this meeting, except that he did not walk up and down the aisle's. To have done so was an impossibility, unless he had walked on the heads of the people.

There was not a cubic inch of vacant ground space anywhere. People clambered up the rails of the pulpit, sat on the steps leading from one pew to another in the gallery, and scores struggled in vain at the entrance to the chapel to get within bearing distance. The atmosphere was excessively oppressive but the man who seemed to feel it least, or to feel it not at all, was the man who worked the hard as the pale faced young revivalist. Women fainted and had to be carried out while He was speaking, but he went along with the same smile on his face. "Don't take them out; don't take them out," he pleaded. "Let them go on their knees and ask for forgiveness. That is the sovereign remedy."

Having spoken for over an hour, he asked the assembly to sing, and someone started "Gwaed y Groes sy'n codi fyny." There was, not sufficient spirit in the singing to please Evan Roberts, and he asked them to sing the hymn again. Immediately the refrain was repeated for the last time a young woman,who seemed to be greatly excited, stood up in a pew, and, turning her back on the missioner, addressed the people in the rear part of the chapel. What she said could not be understood where I was sitting, and she seemed to be oblivious of her surroundings. She was still speaking when the stentorian voice of a man drowned that of the woman. He was singing, 'Duw mawr y rhyfeddodau maith,' and the congregation promptly joined him and sang the tuneful old hymn with thrilling fervour.

Without any invitation, a young woman came forward to the "set fawr," and, going on her knees, made a piteous appeal for forgiveness. The impression produced was intense, and her voice was drowned in a sudden chorus of "amens."

Then an elderly woman stood up in her pew. She also prayed, and was remarkably eloquent. Strong, rough-looking men, who had hitherto showed no signs of emotion, now took up their handkerchiefs, and wept bitterly. One of these shrieked "amen" again and again in a shrill voice, which was weird and piercing. The scene was a memorable one. With greater enthusiasm than ever "Mae addewid Nef o'm hochr" and the repetitions of the refrain, "Pwy a wyr na wrendy clustiau?" became so numerous, and the feeling growing so intense, that people here and there were seen to be impatient to take some part in the service.

O man arose from his seat and made gesticulations, but could not make himself heard. His voice was choked with weeping and he had to sit down without having spoken a single word. Then every man and woman joined simultaneously, some praying, others singing, and others again, endeavouring to speak. All this while Evan Roberts sat in the "set fawr," clapping his hands and exhorting the people to go on. The enthusiasm and ecstatic fervour of the meeting were evidently delightful to him.

After a large number of people had confessed their belief, the meeting closed at 11.30, a very old woman pronouncing the Benediction.

Chapter 7 - The Wesley of Whales

PONTYCYMMER, Thursday, November 17.

That the religious revival is increasing its scope and embracing more and more of the people of Wales was plainly demonstrated by the remarkable services held at Pontycymmel tonight. Never before in the history of the Garvi Valley have such services been seen. Mr. Evan Roberts, to whom the title, of "The Wesley of Wales" is now generally applied, and the young ladies from Loughor who accompany him were early astir, and between five o'clock and 5.30 were on the road, intercepting the night-shift, men returning to their homes from the collieries and inviting them cordially to a prayer meeting to be held at 7.30. There was no need, however, for any invitation to be extended to these miners, for the remarkable experiences at Pontycymmer on Wednesday night were the sole topic of discussion throughout the day.

There was a large attendance at the morning prayer meeting, and all who were present will long remember the fervour of the meeting. Almost everyone present loudly raised his or her voice in praise. Another prayer meeting held in the afternoon was characterised by the same deep religious feeling.

Long before the hour at which the evening service was to commence great crowds of people from all parts of the Garw Valley and the surrounding districts, including a large number from Bridgend, belonging to all denominations and no denomination at all, had flocked to Bethel Calvinistic Methodist Chapel, and hundreds failed to obtain admission.

The meeting opened quietly, but there was a subdued feeling which gradually found expression in various ways. The singing of "Diolch iddo" \("Thanks to Him ") was repeated over and over again. Mr. Roberts then invited the people, with his peculiar wave of the hand, to accept the eternal grace which was freely offered to all, and, finding little response read with great effect a few verses from the Book of Revelation, commented with, "I saw a large multitude which no one could number." He interspersed the reading with appropriate remarks, and before he had completed the passages someone near the door said that an old lady had fainted, and he could not get her out. Then someone in the gallery struck up "Lead, Kindly Light," in Welsh to the tune of "Sandon," and the refrain was taken up with remarkable enthusiasm and repeated several times. This was followed by the rendering of "Eto unwaith mi ddyrchefais," to the tune of "Llanidloes." Before this was finished "Throw out the life-line" was struck up from the gallery, and the rendering of this had a remarkable effect on the congregation. The Rev. J. T. Rees, Pontycymmer, offered a most impressive prayer, asking for a downpour of the Holy Spirit, especially on the young people. The responses were general, and disclosed intense feeling. "Showers of blessing" was followed by "Ni fuasai genyf obaith," a female in the audience repeating the refrain. Another woman struck up "A welsoch chwi Ef?" which was the means of further intensifying the feeling.

The Rev. Mr. Evans, Blaengarw, then offered prayer, in the course of which he remarked that they were too moist with the Heavenly dew to be damned. Miss Cranogwen Mess, the well-known lecturer, who has taken an active part in connection with the services, followed with an eloquent appeal to the young people on the subject, "Place your trust in Jesus."

Mr. Roberts then resumed the conduct of the meeting, smilingly inviting all to receive the great and eternal fortune offered them. From all parts of the building cries could be heard from penitents, With tears coursing down their cheeks, they declared their acceptance of the offer. Prayers were invited, and a middle-aged man under the gallery immediately responded. There was no half-heartedness about the prayer. The man's eyes were closed, his fists clenched, higher end higher rose the voice, supplicating, entreating, bursting now into agony, now into overwhelming grief. Then a question was asked which created a convulsion throughout the building. "Who will accept Jesus?" exclaimed a young wife. Another shouted "Diolch, diolch!" The enthusiasm now was unbounded. Rough, uneducated colliers spoke with a fluency that nothing could check. A middle-aged woman sitting in the aisle declared, "I have fallen as low as it is possible for anyone to fall, and He has received me. Come unto Him all of you." A chorus of "Amens" followed, and the majority of the congregation burst into tears. A large number now announced their conversion, some shouting, "O Arglwydd, cymer fi!" \("O God, take me!"). At eleven o'clock the meeting had not lost any of its fervour.

What was to follow was even more remarkable, and at a quarter-past twelve the enthusiasm was maintained to the fullest degree. A large number of new converts was announced, and after each confession the congregation would burst into singing "Diolch iddo byth am gofio llwch y llawr," which was repeated on some occasions a dozen times. Ministers of the Gospel were to be seen weeping for joy, and prayer after prayer went forth on behalf of some of the penitents. One of the penitents was an old man in the eighties. Shortly after stop-tap a man slightly under the influence of drink entered the chapel, and immediately prayers were offered on his behalf. One of the young ladies who accompanied Mr. Roberts rendered the solo, "Calon Ian," the chorus of which was sung over and over again. Another of the young ladies, who was formerly a school teacher, came across one of her old pupil's, who is now working underground at Pontycymmer, and he became a convert.

Within the past fortnight two very remarkable cases of conversion have occurred. The first was that of a collier whose besetting sin was excessive fondness for the drink, and who seldom attended a place of worship. One night last week he went to the lobby of the Baptist Chapel, and the noise he made there attracted the attention of the minister, the Rev W. Saunders, who went out to see what was happening. This man was there in a state of great mental perturbation, and when spoken to by the minister said that he wished to confer with him privately. Mr. Saunders took the man into his private room attached to the chapel, and there full and ample confession of sin was made. "The black clouds of the Day of Judgement are hanging over me," he said, "and I want to live a better life." Minister and penitent knelt in prayer there and then, and the man has now for all his old haunts and lives up to the standard of a good, respectable citizen.

Then on Wednesday evening, while Mr. Evan Roberts was holding a service at the Tabernacle Chapel, a Church meeting was being held by the officers of the Methodist Church in the village. Here, again, the Rev. W. Saunders was summoned from outside, and, going out, he was approached by one of the most notorious characters in the Garw Valley. He was taken into the minister's private room and asked what his message was. The man first took out a card of membership of one of the local institutions, and said, "I want you to burn that first of all." Mr. Saunders hesitated, and asked the man if he was quite determined in his desire.

"Yes," he replied, "burn it, and don't look at it. Here are three more cards; burn these also, I have felt terribly uneasy within me since I heard you preach a fortnight ago, and I can't go on in this way any longer." After a prayer, this man said that he had called at a public-house for a pint of beer but he could not put his hand to touch it. "I tried my best to take it in my hand, but it was no use, and I left it on the counter before coming here."

Chapter 8 - Greatest Day of His Life

PONTYCMMER, Friday, November 18.

Evan Roberts will be leaving Pontycymmer tomorrow morning. Since he came to the village on Wednesday he has revolutionised its religious and social life as no man has ever done before. The effects of his work are visible everywhere. Nothing else is talked about but the revival, and Evan Roberts's name is on every tongue. He is surrounded by people wherever, he goes. Children follow him, and find a new joy in life by talking to him or touching his hand. He has had only one hour's sleep since he has been in the village, but his vigour and enthusiasm are undiminished.

When I called upon him this afternoon he looked as fresh as if he had been resting like any other man. His health is excellent. Mrs. Maddocks, who is his hostess, told me that he eats very little food, and she never knows when to expect him to his meals. There was a gentleman from Cardiff in the house at the time I called, and be was pressing Mr Roberts to come to the Welsh Metropolis and hold a meeting or meetings in the Torrey-hall.

"I prayed this morning," said the young revivalist, "but there was no bidding for me to go to Cardiff. and until I receive a message from God I shall not go there."

What is your programme for the future?"

I asked him. "I don't know," be replied, except that I go to Bridgend tomorrow and to Abercynon for the whole of next week."

"Have you heard anything from the Methodist authorities to the effect that you are to cease your work as a revivalist?"

"No. I don't want to say anything on the subject except that I don't believe they will interfere with me, a surmise which, I understand, is confirmed by Methodist leaders in your columns."

When asked to relate some of his most stirring experiences Mr. Roberts shook his head and, after a long pause, said: "I would rather not speak. I want to keep myself in the background.01-!"

"Is it true that no watch you carry will keep time?"

"Yes; that is perfectly true. No watch will keep time with me."

In the course of a general conversation Mr. Roberts remarked that the press had been of great assistance, and added, "Especially the 'Western Mail.' They have been very good."

He also said that Thursday was the greatest day of his life. It appears that some remarkable scenes were witnessed at a prayer meeting yesterday morning. Mr. Maddocks, the young revivalist's host, told me that he remembered tile revival of 1859.

"It was nothing like this one," he said. "I never saw such a thing as that prayer meet yesterday morning. Mr Roberts fell prostrate, and remained with his face on the floor for some time, He seemed to be in agony. I shall never forget the meeting. Then, between midnight and two o'clock this morning the state of feeling in the service was quite beyond imagination. One young man who had come from a dance stood up before the end of the meeting and made open confession. Scores of notorious drunkards were there, and they are now changed men."

Speaking to one of the people prominently identified with the revival, Evan Roberts made this remarkable statement:

"When I go out to the garden I see the devil grinning at me, but I am not afraid of him; I go into the house, and, when I go out again to the back I see Jesus Christ smiling at me. Then I know all is well."

Four young ladies who had come under the spell of the "Welsh Wesley," and who were not religiously disposed prior, to this week, are now full of zeal and enthusiasm One of them is a beautiful singer, and she and three others banded themselves together and made a round of the public-houses and the clubs, where they sang hymns and induced men who were drinking there to come to the meeting at Bethel.

I used to go to dances," said one of them. "and I thought I could never give it up, but I shall never go to a dance again." She spoke these words at the close of the afternoon prayer meeting. Evan Roberts was there, and he was observed to be weeping like a child.

The whole village, if not, indeed, the entire Garw Valley, is in a maelstrom of religious emotion. From two o'clock until nearly four o'clock this morning a large number of men grouped together and broke the stillness of the night with song. The few people who were in their beds were awakened by that thrilling melody:

Calon lan yn Ilawn daoni Tecach yw na'r lili dloss;Dim ond calon Ian all ganu.Canu'r dydd a chanu'r nos.

At five o'clock this morning Mr. Roberts was at the pithead waiting for the night shift to come up from below. When the men appeared he shook hands with them all, and invited those of them who were not too tired to come to the prayer meeting. Most of them came. Stirring scenes were witnessed, strong men of rough exterior sobbing almost hysterically, and bearing testimony in quiver broken accents.

Ostensibly, all this commotion is the result of the plain, simple appeals made by Evan Roberts the man without the remotest claim to the title of orator. His language, even, is extremely colloquial and it cannot be truthfully said that what he says is above the common-place. Wherein, then, lies the charm of the man and his power? Perhaps the best answer is that he has an indefinable something in his manner and style. His joyous smile is that of a man in whom there is no guile. His genuineness is transparent, and he convinces people that the belief in what he preaches is impregnable. His restlessness is marvellous he is walking about all day with the springiness of a man treading on wires, his arms swaying unceasingly. He is proof against weariness or fatigue.

"Is your health good?" I asked him. "Oh, splendid," he said, with a smile. "I was never better in my life."

Imagine a man who has had only an hours sleep since Wednesday addressing such a meeting as that held at Bethel in the evening. The chapel was crowded, and the atmosphere stifling. The people seemed to be piled up in one huge mass nearly an hour before the meeting was due to begin. Seeing that press was so great at Bethel, Evan Roberta asked that the Tabernacle Chapel should be opened: This was done, and the building was filled at once. Mr. Roberts addressed this meeting first, and the people in Bethel had to wait for him. No one conducted the service in the orthodox way, but this made no difference. Leadership was not wanted. There was a constant unbroken flow of song, prayer and exhortation from young men alone. The meeting was seething with enthusiasm.

An old man, an octogenarian, rose in the "set fawr" and shouted out in ecstasy, "Diolch, diolch i'r Nefoedd." It was only with great effort He unburdened himself, his final words in Welsh being, "We thank Heaven for this awakening in Wales, but Heaven ought to be gracious to Wales because there are hundreds of Welshmen there."

Intensity of feeling was almost at breaking point when some man who sat in the front gallery gave a vivid description of a drowning man being saved by a comrade. He was about to point the moral when a young lady started singing,

Throw out the life-line, throw out the life-line, Someone is sinking to-day.

The effect was dramatic. The enthusiasm with which the refrain was repeated again and again was uplifting. For some of the "weaker vessels" the effect was too much, and women had to be carried out in a state of collapse. But the tide only rose to its full height when

Marchog Iesu yn Ilwyddiannus

was sung to the tune of "Ebenzer," or more popularly known as "Ton y Botel." The balance of parts was suggestive of a trained choir, and perfect intonation, coupled with the huge volume of song, made the rendering majestic. The hymn was sung at the request of Evan Roberts, who made his appearance at Bethel a little before nine o'clock.

Striking scenes were enacted among the hundreds of people congregated outside the chapel. Three or four hundred assembled in front of the Pontycymmer Hotel, one of the largest licensed houses in the village, and sang "Diolch iddo" and other familiar hymns, and the scene was one of great impressiveness.

To attempt to adequately describe the scenes which marked the meeting at Ebenezer Chapel, Trecynon, during the early hours of Friday morning would be a futile task, and the nearest approach to a due portrayal thereof would be the statement that men and women had become helpless victims to religious fervour. To employ a forcible remark which was used by one of the local ministers, who was present. "The incident was the embodiment of emotional pain which has so overcome the people that they were quite unconscious of the manner in which they unburdened themselves of their overemotion." There can exist no doubt that the movement has penetrated into the very marrow, for prayer services were being held at the outside villages long before nine o'clock on Friday morning.

A well-known Atheist, named Tom Hughes, of Trecynon, got up at the meeting at Ebenezer Chapel, and said that during the day he had burned all his books. Then he went on his knees and prayed fervently for a very long time. In the course of his prayer he earnestly counselled all those persons, who, as he himself had done, were reading those Atheistical books to discard them forthwith, and to follow his example by embracing the faith.

Chapter 9 - Bridgend and Abergwynfi

ABERGWYNFI, Sunday, November 23.

The spirit of the revival is spreading, and there is now ample evidence of the accuracy of the statement which I made on Wednesday that the Churches of all denominations were, and for a time had been, waiting, watching, and praying for the wave which now seems sweeping over the southern half of the Prince of Wales. The visits of Mr. Evan Roberts and his singing evangelists appear to be merely what he himself so aptly described them, "opening the doors" of the revival, for the work which is carried on by others is becoming vast in its extent and wonderfully effective in its operations. People who attend his meetings get "fired" with the zeal of the revival, and proceed to the neighbourhoods in which they live and spread the "infection" wherever they go not only in the Churches, but in the works, in the streets, in the trains, and the subject has become, especially in the mining valleys, the principal topic of conversion among all classes of the community.

One excellent feature of the movement is its absolute freedom from sectarianism and the absence of any attempt at proselytism. The only gospel promulgated is the gospel of love, and the most effective sermon heard on Sunday, beyond question, was the performance of a young girl, with a beautiful voice, at Abercynon, singing with the most, thrilling pathos:

"Dyma gariad fel y moroedd,
Tosturiaethau fel y lli;
T'wysog bywyd pur yn marw
Marw i brynu'n bywyd ni;
Pwy all beidio coflo am dano?
Pwy all beidio canu Ei glod?
Dyma destyn na'd a'n anghof
Tra bo'r Nefoedd wen yn bod."

It was all the more effective because the words and the music expressed the thoughts of all, and because the hymn expresses, in eight lines, the real gist of the gospel of this revival,

But, in order to give some chronological order to this account of Saturday's and to's principal gatherings, let me just glance at the movements of Mr. Roberts and his immediate supporters. From Pontycymmer he went on Saturday to Bridgend. It was market day, and there was a large influx of people from the outlying districts, so the Town-hall was filled by half-past ten, and there was no difficulty in keeping the proceedings going, although (as is the case at the opening meeting in most of the places visited) there was what was described as a coldness which was not completely broken through for some time. Various well-known local people took part, and towards the close a very fervent spirit prevailed, but no converts declared themselves. It was the usual gathering with no consecutive order in the doings, and the incidents were not remarkable when compared with what has occurred elsewhere.

But when Mr. Evan Roberts had left for Pyle and taken with him that is, they follow him apparently all the prominent lay and ministerial elements of the place, there were extraordinary scenes enacted at that same Town-hall at Bridgend. Shortly after two o'clock in the afternoon there stood at, the side door of the hall two young men and five young ladies singing the touching lines

"Calon lan yn llawn daioni,
Perffaith fel y lili dios;
Dim ond calon lan all gana,
Canu'r dydd a chanu'r nos."

I entered, and found the Town-hall absolutely empty, but, I was quickly followed by the singers, and gradually by people from the street, and to hear and see the service that was conducted by these young people, alone and unaided except as they were, as they prayed, "directed by the Spirit" was a sight, which I shall never forget. A workman, who came and sat near me in his working clothes, remained untouched until one of the young women sang. "What a Friend we have in Jesus," and he cried, "Yes, He is my friend, too," and the 'Diolch iddo'which resounded through the half empty hall, must have carried a message to the streets, for the crowd grew and grew until, between half-past three and four, there was a very large audience. Three converts were made, and by the time the visitors had to leave for Abergwynfi one of the preachers from Pyle, after hearing of the gathering, returned and took up the work.

At, Pyle the chapel was not overcrowded, but it was a Saturday after-noon meeting, and the place was not so well calculated too attract outsid-ers as the populous mining district. Yet it was here that Mr. Evan Roberts proved that an injustice has been done him by me and others in the press. It has been said that he is not gifted with eloquence, and that he has no pretensions to oratory. Well, he has no pretensions, it's true. But these later services show that his "visions" are remarkable, not only in their in-fluence upon himself, but in their influence, when related by him, upon others as well. The dramatic incident of Pyle will rank with the highest efforts of the silver-tongued, poetic. imaginative preacher of the Welsh pulpit.

Mr. Roberts had spoken calmly, deliberately, upon his work, and dwelt upon the "love of Christ which passeth all understanding," when he suddenly asked, "Is there no one here who will confess Christ?" A young man falteringly got up, and, after cheering him with the remark that no one need be ashamed to confess Christ, Mr. Roberts said. "Strange that we are so weak as to be unable to face a few, like we have here, to acknowl-edge Jesus Christ!" He then went on, with his eyes fixed upward. "I see a vision. I can see the King of Kings on His Throne I can see around Him, on each side of Him, and behind Him, a vast throng myriads of saints. an-gels, seraphim and cherubim and before that Throne stands our elder brother, Jesus. He stands there, and boldly acknowledges us acknowledges you and me in the presence of that vast assembly. Jesus does not falter. Jesus is not, afraid. Jesus is not ashamed. Yet we very often are afraid or ashamed, or too weak, to stand up before a few people to acknowledge the Saviour Who died for us.'

The effect was remarkable.

Just one other touch, and I shall have done with the Pyle meeting. Speaking of the work that is being done, Mr. Roberts joyously clapped his hands and shouted, "Aha, aha," but remarked that this sort of thing could not go on for ever in this fever-heat could not be kept going long, but let them keep it going as long as they could; I let them keep it going with a swing (which he illustrated with a swing of his right arm) to raise the Churches to a higher level, and then they could "settle down to business." The convert's at Pyle numbered fifteen, and two more actually declared themselves at Tondu Station.

From Pyle to Abergwynfi Mr. Evan Roberts went on Saturday eve-ning, and was there joined by the young men from Loughor and the young ladies from the Bridgend Town hall meeting. The crowded congregation was not as sympathetic at first as might have been anticipated, knowing how the people of the adjoining district have been caught by the "fire" of the revival; but as the time wore on there were remarkable scenes of excitement and enthusiasm. Mr. Evan Roberts appealed for active workers in the Churches. He declared that God does not want idle people. "Are you not prepared," he asked, "to take off your coats?" and immediately a young collier in the gallery got up and actually pulled off his coat, which he threw upon his seat, declaring himself ready for work. The incident created great excitement, and was the means of arousing several others to respond to the call figuratively, though not so literally as the young man already mentioned.

Seeing the Abergwynfi meeting in full swing, after counting 27 converts, Mr. Roberts and his party proceeded to Abercynon, ready for today's meetings, and the torch which had ignited the blaze at Abergwynfi was taken to the Sunday's scene of operations. Tabernacle Chapel at Abercynon was crowded even before Mr. Evan Roberts appeared this morning, but the service seemed too much like the ordinary Sunday service to lead one to expect what soon followed.

I have already referred to the "sermon" conveyed in the wonderfully touching hymn rendered by one of the young ladies. It was not the first incident of the meeting, but it was "the sermon." for Mr. Evan Roberts did not preach a sermon. The gentleman who read a portion of Scripture read it with the spirit of one "touched by the Living fire." The congregational singing was at, times very effective. But "the sermon" contained in that pathetic hymn caught the congregation and swayed it considerably with emotion. Tue missioner (Mr. Roberts) in the course of his address spoke very solemnly of the value of a soul the purchase price, he said, of one soul was the Divine blood. He declared that he had, like others, in the past been more or less imbued with the spirit of anxiety for material position, for an easy retirement from active life and so forth, but he had now given all to God, and did not trouble to look ahead. The God which called for these things was the God Who could provide for all. He had among the letters received last night one containing a cheque for one guinea, the donor asking him not to refuse it. Refuse it, no! He took it for God and would use it for God's work. Another letter told him to write if he wanted money; so that God opened hearts to provide, and he had absolutely no care for the future. Some people, he said, strained their eyes to look ahead, and did not see or smell the beautiful flowers at their feet. Then he came to a climax in relating a, simple incident. While listening to a sermon at

Newcastle-Emlyn once, he said, he received much more of the spirit of the Gospel from what he saw than from what he heard. The preacher was doing very well, was -warming with his work, and sweating by the very energy of his delivery. And when he (Evan Roberts) saw the sweat on the preacher's brow he looked beyond and saw another vision: his Lord sweating the bloody sweat in the garden (and then as Mr. Roberts thought of the "vision" he utterly broke down). The congregation sang "Diolch iddo," and presently Mr. Roberts recovered sufficiently to proceed. On this occasion he invited those who were saved to stand on their feet. The majority of the congregation did so. He then invited those who wished to "confess Jesus" to rise, and several responded. He urged his friends to take down the names, and presently he and others spoke earnestly and privately to a number of others who had not risen. They were not in all cases successful, but at the morning service the new roll-call numbered nineteen, among them being people from Ynyshir, Ynysybwl, Pontypridd, Treharris, and other places. Thus is the "fire" spread.

In the afternoon the meeting was held at the Welsh Congregational Chapel, one of the largest sacred buildings in the town, and the accommodation even then was quite inadeate, and an overflow meeting was held at Bethania. A pathetic rendering of a Welsh hymn was given by Miss Stevens, who broke down, but Quickly recovered herself. Mr. Roberts spoke for over an hour, and remarked that, although some people laughed and scorned at the movement, he did not mind, and trusted in the Holy Spirit.

Chapter 10 - At Mountain Ash

MOUNTAIN ASH, Monday, November 21.

Contrary to his original intention not to go to Mountain Ash until next Saturday, Mr.Evan Roberts arrived at that place shortly after ten o'clock this morning, in obedience, he said, to a summons he had received from the Holy Spirit during his stay at Abercynon. Although the news of his coming was only slightly known, large throngs of people had congregated at the railway station to receive the young revivalist and his lady supporters, who proceeded at once to Bethlehem Welsh Calvinistic Methodist Chapel, where a service was held forthwith. The building was quickly crowded to its utmost capacity. The service was opened with a fervent rendering of the hymn, "A welsoch chwi Ef" \("Have you seen Him?")

After numerous repetitions of the few closlines, Mr. Roberts proceeded to address the congregation. According to his wont, he walked to and fro. In a deep voice he briefly narrated the history of the revival, which, he said, with a solemn look upwards, was the outcome of a call from God to His people on earth. To him no credit was due for the great manifestations of religious awakening which was traversing the country, for he was only giving vent to the devotional fire which had been instilled into him by the Divine Hand.

No sooner had the last words fallen from his lips than the tall form of a young lady. was seen in the gallery, and the gathering was thrilled with the singing of "O rest in the Lord." It was a stimulating and effective rendering, the singer being Miss Rachel Ann Thomas, a well-known soprano. The emotion was now at its highest point, and the congregation was evidently under some spell which it would be futile to try to describe.

Owing to the large number of people who had congregated outside the chapel for the afternoon service, it was decided to hold an overflow meeting at Bethania. Both buildings were crowded long before the time of starting, and Mr. Roberts, after speaking for a few minutes at Bethlehem, went to the other place, where he spoke in the same terms as at the morning service. The proceedings were marked with great fervour, and were interspersed with spontaneous prayers and singing. "Dyma gariad lel y moroedd" ("Here is love in copious torrents") was sung, with telling effect.

In the evening three meetings were held, but, owing to the limited accommodation, hundreds of persons were obliged to returns to their homes. What has been said as to gatherings in other places may be repeated with regard to the beginning of the revival movement at Mountain Ash. On all hands it is said that the "fire" has been smouldering for a long time, and that the great outburst could not be long deferred.

In the course of a conversation the Rev. D. Anthony, pastor of Providence Chapel, Mountain Ash, said the movement was only in its infancy, and before long there would be such a wave of religious awakening as the world had not seen for a long time, as the atmosphere was charged with it.

Chapter 11 - A voice from Macedonia

MOUNTAIN ASH, Tuesday, November 22.

Not only is the religious revival going on with vigour and zeal wherever Mr. Evan Roberts appears, but the "fire" is spreading amazingly where he has been, and also among people in districts from which visitors have attended Mr. Roberts's meetings. News from Aberdare is that there were no fewer than a dozen great meetings being held during to-day and evening in Aberdare alone, and from Porth and Pontypridd come tidings of a new life in Churches which are seemingly in no way directly connected with the movements of Mr. Evan Roberts.Yet it is unquestionable that, although he is not the actual cause of the revival, his movements and his indirect influence inspire others to help forward the realisation, of the yearnings with which so many of the Churches are possessed for greater spiritual life and activity.

At Trecynon and Aberdare the revival inaugurated by Mr. Roberts's mission increased immensely in power during this week, although Mr. Roberts has not been there since last Wednesday. The communion service at the Welsh Congregational Chapel, Aberdare, on Sunday last is described as the most impressive ever known to have been held within the memory of anyone present. At Heol-y-felin, Aberdare, arrangements have been made for what will, undoubtedly, be an extraordinary and impressive sight next Sunday when between 90 and 100 adults will be publicly baptised by immersion. At Aberthe great gatherings held on Monday and Tuesday were inspiring in their fervour.

And while these things are going on all around Mr. Evan Roberts continues his unostentatious mission in Mountain Ash, drawing on Tuesday crowds which overcrowded Bethel Chapel and its vestry, and filled the English Presbyterian and Welsh Congregational Chapels all three at the same time. He was present at Bethania (Congregational) in the morning, and the service was an exceedingly important one, the "arddeliad' of the Spirit, as it is so idiomatically described, being remarkable.

In the afternoon, at Bethel Chapel, the scenes which were enacted were different in many respects from those which have been witnessed elsewhere. Some of the hearers were so moved by the prayers of others as to rise to their feet and shout, the interjections being running comments on the prayers themselves, but it was more like the "hwyl" of a great "cymanfa" that the usual Welsh fire elicited by these revival meetings, It partook more of the "sot fawr" element. Still, there was great enthusiasm, and Mr. Evan Roberts himself said he was a different man from Monday, when he felt somewhat depressed. To-day he was buoyant in spirit, and in the coarse or his address once more laid stress on the absolute necessity for relying not upon him, nor upon any human being, but upon the Spirit. Later on he dwelt upon the importance of praying for a baptism of the Spirit, to infuse life and to invest each person with some power to work for the Lord.

In the evening, when the three meetings to which I have already referred were held simultaneously, there were some striking scenes enacted. At Bethel there was at first an apparent lack of voluntary service in prayer, and the response to Mr. Evan Roberts's appeal for prayers on behalf of the two young men who had gone to start a meeting at Tyntetown was somewhat slow, the intervals, however, being filled with Hymn singing. Suddenly there stood up in the aisle a man attired in corduroy, who bore powerful testimony to the value of religion and prayed that the influence of the revival might spread across the border to England. Later on a young Turk elbowed his way to the front and managed to send a note to Mr. Evan Roberts, When the note had been read Mr. Roberts asked the friends to invite the young foreigner to the platform, but before introducing him to the congregation asked the huge assembly, "Would you like to hear a cry from Macedonia?" and when the surprise had given way to cries of "Amen" Mr. Roberts said, "You shall hear it now!" The congregation began singing "Dioich iddo," and when the singing ceased the stranger began, in broken English, but otherwise with a wonderful flow of words and thoughts, to explain the pleasure he felt at being permitted, as a saved Turk, to give his testimony to people who had the privilege of living in a Christian land. He stated that he first heard of the love of a crucified Christ from a young black girl from Macedonia in his own country in Turkey.

Proceeding to give illustrations of matters which created surprise in his mind in this country, he said some people in this "land of the Bible" dared to say that there was no God. In one instance, he said, when he was working in the coal pit at Cilfynydd, Pontypridd, he had as a fellow-workman one of such men. When he (the speaker) prayed, as he usually did, before partaking of his meal, that man asked him, "What good has that done you?" his reply was, "No good to my body, but I am better in Spirit." Presently he heard the timbers crash. There was a scream, and the colliers present would understand what he meant by that scream. Men rushed to the face of the coal, and then the first he heard crying out "Lord, save me, was a man who just previously had said that there was no God. The man who had been injured asked him (the speaker) to tell the man's wife to bring up their children in the religion of this converted Turk, as he (the father) had lived. There were men who fought against this movement to-day, and against the spread of the Christian religion, but God would remove the stumbling-blocks. He then gave illustrations of the good that could he done by private conversations more could be done by a simple act of kindness than by public speaking or even singing. The Turk then sang an English hymn, in the refrain of which the vast assembly heartily joined. Then he made another startling statement, startling in more than one sense. He said he would sing a verse of the same hymn in his own Turkish language, because there might be one or two Turks present who did not understand either Welsh or English. "It was surprising," he said, "what numbers of them were scattered here and there in the collieries." He then sang the Turkish hymn, the refrain being taken up by the audience in English.

One man in the audience fervently prayed the Lord to move the people in those crowded congregations to go out into the streets of Mountain Ash to sing the Gospel into the hearts of sinners, and there was every evidence that before the night was over the suggestion would be carried into effect.

I ought to have mentioned earlier that during the afternoon a lady in the congregation asked for prayers for the spread of the revival to Llantrisant, and she then sang the sweet hymn, "To save a great sinner like me."

It was understood that Mr. Evan Roberts would confine his services to Bethel Chapel at night, but during the interval he suddenly disappeared from the platform, and was away from the meeting for some time. When I left, in order to visit the English Methodist Chapel and Bethania, I met Mr. Evan Roberts in the street, bareheaded, in the cold, snowy air, returning from a surprise visit to the English Methodist Chapel, "Mae'r Ysbryd yn, eu plith nhw" ("The Spirit is among them"), he said. When quietly reminded of the danger of going about bareheaded on such, a cold night he smilingly said, "I don't think of it," and immediately returned to Bethel Chapel, where he infused his own energy once more into the proceedings.

Chapter 12 - Sweeping like a wave

YNYSYBWL, Wednesday, November 23.

"Sweeping like a wave" over the mining districts of Glamorganshire, the Welsh revival is overwhelming places which have not been visited by Mr. Evan Roberts. Not only in the towns and villages which I yesterday referred to, but in others around, strange scenes are daily enacted, indicating not merely the intense longing for a spiritual revival among the Churches, but the actual presence of a spirit of religious fervour which rouses people to unwonted activity. At Porth (where the Rev. R. B. Jones is on a mission) meetings are held in various chapels during the daytime. At Havod similar gatherings are attended with great success. From the Great Western Colliery comes news of an extraordinary character that prayer meetings have been held there underground for over a week!

Those who attended the earlier portions of Mr. Evan Roberts's meeting at Mountain Ash can have but a faint notion of the work done during the late hours of last night, for the congregation were only thoroughly aroused about eleven o'clock at night. Then, as denoting the way in which the "fire" is spread, it is as well to mention that at Mountain Ash and Abercynon Stations there were services held on the platforms while people were waiting for their trains to depart homewards.

The visit of Mr. Evan Roberts to Ynysybwl was anticipated at that place by a strange awakening among the young people, many of them who had never, probably, prayed bofore having during the past week been prompted by the Spirit for they were not invited or urged by minister, deacons, or members to take public part in the ordinary services. Then this morning there was a largely attended meeting at Jerusalem Chapel, and a, very successful service was carried on, although Mr. Roberts did not arrive until the two o'clock train. When he arrived another meeting had been commenced, and the chapel was simply overcrowded from pulpit to doors, along the aisles, in the lobby, and on the pulpit stairs. The address delivered by Mr. Roberts was an impressive one, and when he commended the proceedings to the care of the Spirit there were some remarkable testimony given and especially the news given of the spread of the revival in

Cwmpark. The young man who gave this information said he had come to that meeting to hear Evan Roberts, but he thanked God that, he had heard someone greater than Evan Roberts that day. "Diolch iddo," shouted Mr. Roberts, joyfully, and there followed some enthusiastic hymn-singing. Miss Annie Davies, of Maesteg, was now accompanied by a number of young ladies from Mountain Ash, who rendered assistance in connection with the pathetic rendering of some of the pieces sung. Miss Davies herself was again wonderfully effective in her extraordinary rendering of "Dyma gariad fel y moroedd" ("Here is love in copious torrents"), and one pecularity of her stirring work ought to be extraordinary. Yesterday when a ministerial gentleman broke down in prayer she continues the fervency by singing in a very low, pathetic voice:

> "O ainfon Di, yr Ysbryd Glan.
> Yn enw'r Iesu mawr,
> A'i ddylanwadau megys tan,
> 0 anfon Ef i lawr."

Later on, when in the midst of a powerful prayer, one man asked the Lord to enable them all to realise the greatness of the sacrifice of Jesus Christ, Miss Davies, very gently and with quivering voice, sang:

> "Dyma gariad fel y moroedd,"

end then she stopped, but presently added the second line,

> "Tosturiaethau fel y lii,"

and there was another pause as if she were playing a touching accompaniment to the heartfelt prayer of the supplicant, The incident was, to me, the most artless and yet most effective feature of the gathering. The same thing happened on Monday, when she punctuated with glorious music the rousing remarks of a speaker who stood in the front of the gallery. Mr. Evan Roberts himself does not at all object to this method of pro and he experienced it to-day, when he smilingly went on with a number of exhortations to the tender accompaniment of music, which was so modified in volume as not to interfere with his voice, but seemed to come from a distance, although in one instance Miss Davies, who sang, was standing at his side.

Mention of the Cwmpark incident reminds me that Mr. Evan Roberts in the course of his address had, dwelt very emphatically upon the absolute neccesity for casting all self and everything human out of the movement, for if success was to be assured all the work must be the spontaneous outcome of the moving of the Spirit.

Then, as confirming what has been said with regard to the spontaneity of the movement in various directions, I was told that over a fortnight ago a ministerial prayer meeting had been held by the Wesleyans of the district, and that the activity and earnestness of the young people were very marked.

The apparent coldness of the first portion of the afternoon meeting had a somewhat depressing effect on Mr. Evan Roberts himself, for his face occasionally became sad.

But later on and at night, when the large chapel was crowded not only to the doors, but when people were standing in crowds outside, there was every evidence of a strong accession of power. Mr. Evan Roberts spoke at some length. After an impassioned address from a speaker who had followed the meetings from Mountain Ash, the great audience, led by a soloist, sang very sweetly and pathetically Sankey's soulful hymn, "Jesus of Nazareth," and it was noteworthy that the service was more typical of the English element than, perhaps, any of the others, except that which was held last night at Duffryn-street English Methodist Chapel, Mountain Ash, when Mr. Roberts himself left Bethel to proceed to the overflow meeting and delivered a very practical address in English. His addresses to-day, however, were in the Welsh language.

The singing was now varied by the render of several voluntary - sacred solos, the refrains of which wore sung with splendid effect.

Chapter 13 - Second Day at Ynysybwl

YNYSYBWL, Thursday, November 24.

The second day's proceedings of the revival meetings conducted at Ynysybwl by Mr. Evan Roberts were marked by extraordinary scenes of religious fervour, and the news from other districts continues to show that the tide is still rising. "Throw out the life-line" is not only being sung, but acted upon. At Ynysybwl the highest expectations are being fulfilled, for from morning until night the gatherings have been large and successful in every sense. The morning meeting at Jerusalem Chapel today began at 10.30, and the spiritual tendencies of the congregation were aroused even before the arrival of Mr. Evan Roberts, but the personal appeals of the missioner in his address focussed the aims of the meeting on securing declarations for Christ rather than merely allowing the already converted to sing songs of praise, good though such work might be.

In the afternoon (when, owing to the announcement made in the "Western Mail," it was generally thought that Mr. Roberts would be in Merthyr) there was a crowded audience in Jerusalem, Ynysybwl, and it is advisable here to explain that the arrangement with regard to the Merthyr meetings had not been ratified by Mr. Roberts or the deacons of the Ynysybwl chapel. It was felt that the flow of the tide of the mission at Ynysybwl might be interfered with if the man whose personality is mainly identified with the revival were to leave so soon, and the Merthyr invitation was,

Before Mr Roberts's arrival the chapel was overcrowded, and an overflow meeting was held in the Weslyan Chapel. When he arrived, shortly before three o'clock, the meeting was well on, the Rev. J. C. Lloyd, Congregational minister, having aroused it to a high pitch of enthusiasm by his leadership of the singing. But the meeting had started well. A man in the gallery had risen and delivered an impassioned appeal to all, but especially to his fellow-workmen, to "come over to the right side." The congregation sang "Diolch iiddo," and when the hymn was-concluded an Abercynon minister rose and exclaimed, "Yes, diolch iddo ('Thank Him'), if it were only for saving the last speaker, He is one of the Abercynon converts." He then explained the difficulty found in getting the last speaker to "break through?" He went away from the first meeting, and was unable to sleep that night, but came voluntarily the next day. He was glad to tell them that the converts at Abercynon now numbered 300.

Mr Roberts utilised as the text of his address the stirring words, "Throw out the life-line." He asked the audience to fully realise the meaning of the words, and consider that there were friends around them, on all sides, who were drifting away or "sinking." The response was prompt and effective, for the beautiful hymn was sung with a heartiness which was very striking.

From this incident onward the zeal and enthusiasm became almost unbounded. hymn after hymn was sung; a prayer, "experience," testimony, appeal, exhortation, solo, duet, or recitation of verse or hymn followed in rapid succession, men, women and children, ministers, laymen all classes taking part, and when Mr. Evan Roberts invited those who were "saved" in that vast congregation to stand up there was a mighty response. Then, from among those seated, at the second invitation for those who wished to be saved to rise, six or seven young men sitting together in one row on the front of the gallery rose, and others stood up in various parts of the building, so that when the rapturous "Diolch iddo" of the congregation broke forth it was like the mighty peal of a great anthem of triumph. The scene was really indescribable. While it was thought some were hesitating Mr. Evan Roberts invited the congregation to sing Newman's hymn, "Lead, kindly Light," and it was pathetically sung in Welsh and English. Then there arose again the inspiring strains of "Throw out the life-line," and there were further responses. The Rev, J. C. Lloyd sang to the tune "Haden," full of rolling slurs and beautiful cadences, an old hymn of days gone by:

> "Dewch, bechaduriaid, dewch,
> Yn filoedd maith diri',
> Ar anghrediniaeth na wrandewech,
> At orsedd freiniol Nef
> Mae croesaw, mae croesaw,
> Mae croesaw i'ch bath chwi;
> Y Gwr bia'r wlad sy'n dwedyd dewch"

And when Miss Annie Davies, of Maesteg, sang her peculiarly pathetic rendering of "Jesus only," there was a totally different style of evangelisation brought into play:

"Os caf Iesu, dim ond Iesu,
Bydd fy Nef yn oleu' i gyd
Bydd fy heulwen wedi codi
Ar fy mywyd yn y byd"

Personal prayer for individuals, in some instances named, were asked for, and in at least one instance the person referred to confessed Christ.

Perhaps one of the most striking incidents of the night meeting was the rendering by Miss Annie Davies of "Dyma Feibl anwyl Iesu," which was given in a remarkably effective and original manner, the young lady herself holding the large pulpit Bible in her arms as she sang. It was announced in the course of the meeting that one of the converts received that night was one for whom prayers had been offered specially in the course of the afternoon, It was confidently expected that at least one other convert would be brought in in the same way in the course of the night, although it was stated that he was supposed to be in a public house in order to avoid coming within the influence of the revival.

The proceedings were protracted until a very late hour, and were not expected to finish till the early hours of the morning.

Chapter 14 - Temporary Indisposition

CILFYNTDD, Friday, November 25.

Although Mr. Evan Roberts was so far exhausted after his labours at Ynysybwl as to be unable to reach Cilfynydd this afternoon, there was an extraordinary meeting in the Calvinistic Methodist Chapel shortly after, two o'clock. To begin with, however, let me say that the revival has been going on in Cilfynydd all the week, and indeed, for some time previously. Several converts have been added to the local Churches at meetings held every night, and the visit of "the missioners" was expected, not to start, but to give additional impetus to the work. The prayer meeting held in the morning was very largely attended, and some converts were enrolled. But this afternoon, when Miss Annie Davies, Maesteg, and her sister, Miss Maggie Davies, and Miss S. K. Jones, of Nantymoel, entered the chapel, the singing became very powerful, and the gathering became a remarkable one in many senses.

The absence of Mr. Evan Roberts was not alluded to publicly, but several visitors afterward privately expressed regret at having been unable to see and hear the man about whom so much has centred in this extraordinary movement. Several of the local ministers were present, and, in so far as any one took charge of The proceedings at all, the conduct of the meeting was in the hands of the pastor of the Church (the Rev. Michael Williams); but very soon men from the gallery and from various parts of the floor of the chapel burst forth in praise and prayer, in exhortation and recital of Scriptural verses. Three or four prayed simultaneously, others sang, and at times it would be impossible to describe the condition of things except as indescribable confusion. And yet, out of seeming chaos would come order, and a pathetic prayer or a touching hymn would once more unite the whole of the vast congregation in one common object. When the congregation stood it was noticed that several remained seated, and Miss Maggie Davies and Miss Jones promptly left the platform to talk and pray with the unsaved. Every now and then the striking up of "Diolch iddo" ("Thanks to Him") indicated another name enrolled, and when special prayers for individuals were called for there were fervent petitions offered in English and Welsh.

Chapter 15 - Every Chapel Filled

PORTH, Sunday, November 27.

Mr. Evan Roberts had so far recovered from his indisposition as to enable him to proceed at mid-day yesterday to Cilfynydd, whither he was accompanied by Miss Davies, of Gorsand the afternoon and evening meetings at that place proved that the work of the revival is still going ahead at a rapid rate.

In the morning, in the absence of Mr. Roberts, there had been a very successful gathering conducted mainly by the Rev. Michael Williams (pastor of the church) and the three young ladies who had arrived the previous day, viz., the Misses Annie and Maggie Davies, of Maesteg, and Miss Jones, of Nantymoel, reinforced by Miss Harries, of Mountain Ash. The proceedings were of practically the same character as those conducted by Mr. Roberts, and it was noticed that among the various classes represented in the gathering were several from distant places.

In the afternoon Mr. Roberts delivered an address of upwards of an hour's duration, in the course of which he emphasised the idea that the members of the Christian Church were all one family. They sank at these meetings, when in the right spirit, all denominations divisions, and met as one family around one hearth. Presently, there was a reference made by one of the speakers to Jesus Christ as a Saviour, and Mr. Roberts again got up, and pointed to the necessity of accepting Christ as King. Some of old had said, "We will not have him to reign over us!" The children accepted Christ as King as well as Saviour. The vast congregation then began singing "Crown Him Lord of All." Another missioner from Merthyr spoke, dwelling upon the significance of the Kingship of Christ, and the recitals of testimonies were very numerous. During the time when the congregation stood to test the meeting for converts Miss Davies, Gorseinon, and Miss Marries specially devoted themselves to quiet talks with waverers in the gallery, and a converted number of names were enrolled.

Miss Maggie Davies, of Maesteg, sang with wonderful effect

Bendithiaist goed y meusydd
O'r brigau hyd y gwraidd
Porthaist y pum mil gwerin
A'r pum torth bara haidd,
Yng Nghana Galilea,
droest y dwr yn win,
O, Dduw, rho im' ollyngdod,
O'm caeth bechhodau blin.

The quaintness of the words and music were very striking, and fully in accordance with the simplicity of the service.

At night, not only was the large chapel filled, but I believe every chapel in Cilfynydd and the neighbourhood were also fairly filled. There was no work at the colliery owing to "stop wagons," and the men certainly very largely availed themselves of the opportunity to attend the revival meetings.

Among those who attended from a distance were the Rev. Penar Griffiths, of Pentre Estyll, who prayed and spoke with great force and earnestness, adding materially to the spiritual character of the gathering. He said he had come there for inspiration for his Sunday's work, and he had received it. He thanked God he had raised a young man to rouse the Churches of his native land and when reading the accounts of the services held in various parts he had felt his heart overflowing with gratitude for having lived to see this great revival wave brought over the hearts of the people by the Spirit of God. In reading the account of the meetings at Trecynon, and the taking of the names of converts, he wondered whether some of his erstwhile companions and men who in their younger days had worked with Him at Nantmelyn Colliery, Aberdare, were on the "saved-list." He hoped they were, and, if not, he [...missing word?...]

Subsequently all eyes were centred on a tall figure, attired in a long robe not unlike Father Ignatius standing in the big seat. The man, who rose to speak, soon got silence, and in the course of a few clearly expressed sentences he said he had come from about 80 miles the other side of London to see and hear the wonderful things that were being done for Christ in Wales. He and others had been for several weeks I think he said two months "praying and fasting" praying four hours a day for God to save souls in Wales, and then at the beginning of this week he began reading paragraphs in the London papers and subsequently full accounts in the South Wales papers of the power with which, God spoke through Evan Roberts to the people of Wales, and of the great work which was being done. The spirit of the revival, he, declared, was spreading into England, and he hoped and prayed that it would extend until it took possession of the whole of Great Britain. The speaker was Mr. M'Taggart, "formerly an Anglo-Catholic, but now only for Christ and for souls," to use the phrase he used himself. The same gentleman visited some of the chapels in the Rhondda on Sunday, and spoke very effectively. I understand that he is a gentleman of position who has given up a considerable amount of his wealth and position in order to devote himself to the work of spreading the truths of the Gospel. He subsequently also (i.e., on Saturday night) spoke to the young men coming out from a Pontypridd public-house, and advised them to go and hear "Evan Roberts, the man of God," who would be at Porth next day. Like Mr. Garett, of Whit who takes a keen interest in this Welsh revival, Mr. M'Taggart has visited the Holy Land in order to be able to speak from greater observation of the scenes associated with the "earthly footsteps of the Man of Galilee" At no meeting which I have yet attended in connection with Mr. Evan Roberts's mission had there been such universal, "testimony" offered as at this great gathering at Cilfynydd. From all parts of the building, simultaneously at times and then in quick sucession, came public confessions of the "love of Christ," and when during an interval Miss Davies, Gorseinon (seeing a struggle going on in the mind of a waverer), struck up "Throw out the life-line," the singing of the congregation became intense in its pathetic earnestness.

At Porhi today Mr. Evan Roberts was not well enough to undertake the morning service at Calfaria. Mss Davies, Gorseinon; Miss S. A. Jones, Nantymoel; and the two sisters from Maesteg the Misses Annie and Maggie Davies and the Rev. Emlyn Jones (pastor of the Church) took charge of the proceedings, and there was upon the whole, an impressive gathering, although the warmth which characterised some of the other meetings seemed to be lacking for a time. The coldness of the weather, doubtless, accounted for this, to some extent, for the meetings held in the other chapels in the afternoon (also in the absence of Mr. Roberts) were very enthusiatic. However, it was not by any means a fruitless meeting, for several converts declared themselves desirous of joining the Churches. Miss Annie Davies, Maesteg, again, sang the Welsh version and my translation of

"Here's a Love like mighty torrents,
Pity like the boundless sea."

This afternoon Mr. Evan Roberts conducted the service at Calfaria, and the congregation filled the chapel and the lobby and occupied the steps outside in the intense cold and overflow meetings were held in the Welsh Congregational Chapel and Bethlehem. At the last-named the evangelists who assisted the Rev. T. P. Thomas were Miss Davies, Gorseinon, and Miss Jones, Nantymoel. In the course of his address the Rev. T. P. Thomas dwelt very strongly upon the great influence wielded by the press in this matter, and declared that hundreds of people wept with joy in reading the very full and sympathetic accounts given of the revival meeting. Reading the accounts had spread the desire for similar gatherings, and had inspired many to go and work for the cause, while it had induced some at least to go to the meetings, and by so doing they had had their souls saved.

To revert to the meeting addressed by Mr. Roberts himself, however, let me say that, undoubtedly, many hundreds had to turn away from the doors, and although, of course, some of these were accommodated at other chapels, there was keen disappointment felt at the fact that only those in one common small chapel could hear, or even see him. True, Mr. Roberts would be the first to say that people should not look to him; but it was felt by very many that it was a great pity one or two of the largest chapels in the town had not been officially announced as the meeting-places.

This was still further accentuated at night. Bethlehem Chapel (Calvinistic Methodist) was the meeting-place, and, obviously, when it was announced at the afternoon service that Mr. Roberts would be there that night it could be seen that the building could not possibly hold one-fourth of the people who would flock to try and hear him. Long before half-past five the chapel was crowded to its utmost limits, and although six o'clock was the time announced for opening the service, the crowds seen turning homeward or to other chapels were immense. A whisper had gone forth that Mr. Roberts would also speak at Salem Baptist Chapel the largest available so I saw Mr. Evan Roberts in order to ascertain whether that would be so, and was told it could not be done. The difficulty of handling the work at two different meetings simultaneously is a great one, and (as Mr. Roberts's host informed me) the doctor has emphatically forbidden the missioner from indulging in the practice of going from one hot meeting to another through the cold night air as he has been doing. The work had, therefore, to be carried on under the disadvantage or addressing a crowded congregation in a small building. The service was of the same character as that which has become typical of the mission, the enthusiasm being very great but the conversions were, comparatively, not so numerous as at other places. Two reasons probably account for that. In the first place, the revival wave had reached a very high level before Mr. Roberts arrived, and scores, if not hundreds, of converts have been enrolled, so that "drawing in the life" could not possibly be expected to show so many immediate results. In the second place, the chapels were crowded at an early hour by people who were mostly members of the different Churches, so that the crowd who had to turn away may have included many who could have been directly benefited by admission.

Chapter 16 - The Revivalist Jubilant

PORTH, Monday, November 23.

Hundreds have seen and heard Mr. Evan Roberts to-day who were unable to gain admittance to the revival meetings on Sunday, and the wave is still rolling on with mighty vigour, while the news pouring in from all sources shows that the converts in different places in the Rhondda and Pontypridd during Sunday must have numbered hundreds. I understand there were forty converts at the Cymmer Independent Chapel on Sunday; that there were numbers at Salem (Baptist); at the hall of the English Baptists, and elsewhere in Porth; while from Pontypridd I hear of 28 at the Welsh Baptist Tabernacle, 60 at the Porth Primitive Methodist Chapel, twelve at the People's hall, nine at the Town-hall (English Baptist), and eight at Calvary, Treforest, and that at Ynysybwl the converts up to the present time number upwards of 400, The "lists" are not yet properly collated in regard to Mr. Evan Roberts's meetings at Perth, but, the "flowing tide" is in the same direction everywhere. I hear that at Treharris there was a great meeting in the "Square" on Saturday night, and that men who had been in public-houses were induced to go to the meetings in the chapels afterwards, and many of them were sobered and converted.

But to come to Porth. There was a morning service at Perth Chapel (Congregational), where the missioner (Mr. Evan Roberts) attended, and the spiritual character of the proceedings may well be described as equal to any that has been held in the Taff and Rhondda districts, In the afternoon the Welsh Independent Chapel, Cymmer, was crowded, and an overflow meeting became absolutely necessary, so the doors of the old chapel on the other side of the road were thrown open, and that was promptly filled when it was understood that Mr. Evan Roberts would call there on his way to the larger chapel. At the old chapel Principal Prys, of Trefecca, was among the audience. At the new chapel Principal Edwards, of Cardiff, sat in the "big pew," and there were many visitors from Cardiff, Penarth, and other places. Mr. Roberts spoke at both chapels, and said when he came to the new chapel that the warmth of the service in the old chapel was refreshing. His address was not so long as the addresses which he has lately delivered, but it was buoyant and practical. "If you have the love of Christ in your heart," he said, "you will love everybody, and you cannot do a mean trick," "If you are not prepared to forgive others, it is no use going on your knees to-night to ask God to forgive your transgressions. I don't say don't do it, Please yourselves, of course, but one thing is certain absolutely certain God will not listen to.

This simple truth is carrying considerable weight, and on all hands I hear of friendships renewed and family feuds ended by hearing the recital of this trite saying. But, to proceed with the meeting, let me say that I felt there was at first too much of the "Cymanfa Ganu" in itset hymns to set tunes, with a well-known conductor leading, Of course, he did his work splendidly, but, as he himself afterwards declared, there might be and there was too much of that style of singing. It was not so spontanious as that which has been witnessed at other place. Still, the volume of sound and the beauty of the harmony were very striking, and between the hymns there were some fervent and eloquent prayers and some remarkable testimonies.

One man in the gallery said he had been a member of the Baptists and a "saved man" since he was fifteen, but he had not received the Holy Ghost into his heart until recently. He said he was not a drunkard, or a swearer, or a bad man in the ordinary acceptation of the term, but the baptism of the Spirit had not come to him until lately. Since then he had, for the first time, conducted family worship in his own house, he had done what he could to tell his fellow-workmen about salvation, and he had gone about the public-houses of the neighbourhood delivering tracts, and was ready to do anything he could.

Another referred to the fact that a young footballer in Cilfynydd had burnt his newly-bought outfit, and offered his season-ticket for international matches to his brother, who burned it, A woman from Mardy declared that she had caught additional fire to go home to Mardy, but she could not be so well satisfied as, perhaps, she ought to be if she did not have an opportunity of shaking hands with Mr. Roberts.

Later on again Mr. Roberts invited Christians publicly to declare themselves, and, swlowly, but surely, came the response. Here and there came one or two, reciting verses; hymns, or making use of their own words; and then from gallery and floor simultaneously came a chorus of voices repeating certain verses together, until at last it was almost impossible to tell who was speaking or what anyone was saying.

Evan Roberts smiled and clapped his hands in joy. "Go on," he said, "don't stop you can all confess Christ at the same time scores of you hundreds of you," and while the excitement was increasing a man from the gallery shouted, "Here is reality! Hear is reality! Thank God!" This state of things continued for some time with an occasional outburst of hymn-singing and "throwing out the life-line." Miss Annie Davies,' Maesteg; was present with her singing Gospel, and the rapt attention given when she sang in Welsh and English,

"Dyma gariad fel y moroedd,"

was only broken by sobs and "Amens," This remarkable meeting continued until after five o'clock and when leaving the chapel with a brother journalist the last words that were literally shouted with joy at us by a man standing in the doorway were, - "Thank God for the press to help the cause of God!"

While this was going on at Cymmer Miss Davies (Gorseinon), Miss Maggie Davies (Maesteg), and Miss Jones (Pontycymmer) were at an Ynyshir chapel a mile and a half away conducting another service, and there, also, there.

But just look at Salem Chapel, the large building of the Welsh Baptists in Hannah -street, Porth. The missioner was announced to speak there at seven o'clock that evening, Therefore, people took their seats in the chapel as early as half-past three o'clock in tho afternoon, and long before the hour fixed for opening the chapel was crowded, and the approaches were thronged with people, while hundreds stood in the streets hoping to get in when any of the others came out, and others merely in the hope of catching a glimpse of Evan Roberts.

Chapter 17 - Converts at Treorky

TREORKY, Tuesday, November 29

The appearance of Mr. Evan Roberts at Treorky to-day was hailed with joy by thousands, and the meeting addressed by him were attended by immense crowds. almost, if not quite, as great as those at Porth on the previous day. It should, how be noted at the outset that the revival appears to have reached "high tide" in the upper part of the Rhondda, prayer meetings having been held nightly for weeks before the wonderful story of the Loughor "fire" was published in the "Western Mail."

The streets to-day were slippery, and in parts dangerous, from the effects of the ice and snow, and the dripping clouds of mist which enveloped the Rhondda hillsides made the roads muddy in places, and in others they were much too smooth. Yet people trudged to Ainon Chapel, at the upper end of Treorky, and filled it literally to over before I reached there in the afternoon For a time I had to content myself with listening from the vestry to the sounds of voices coming through the four doorways behind the rostrum. After a while I managed to work my way in, for I am gaining experience in this difficult task. The meeting was, in a measure, similar to others which I have recently attended. It was decidedly warm, sympathetic, and quite typical of Treorky's active congregations. The hymns were started quite spontaneously, very often by young people and were sung; with fervour and in excellent time. The prayers were earnest, and in many instances marked by simple, but burning eloquence, some of the women being particularly pathetic in their appeals for "wandering boys," and the public confessions by members of churches were extraordinary in character and in number. I think I can safely say that practically all the adult members of the various denominations present and very many children, gave brief testimonies or quotations of Scripture.

But, listen! Mr. Evan Roberts, in one of his incidental addresses, says, "A oes heddwch?" ("Is there peace?") "The question," he said, "is often asked in the eisteddfod. It is quite time that it should be asked in many Churches." He mentioned the topic which I quoted yesterday as to family feuds and personal animosities. Then, he asked, had they ever seen a religious revival in a Church which was torn by dissensions in which members and deacons, or members among themselves, were quarrelling and bickering? Had they seen religious fervour and success in a Church in which the members were cold towards each other? No, never; and the question, "A oes heddwch?" ought to be put wherever there was anxiety to be active for Christ if success did not attend the efforts put forth.

It is a striking truth, and has a practical bearing upon the work of the Christian Churches, as well as upon that of individuals.

Chapter 18 - Drunkards Reformed

TREORKY, Wednesday, November 30.

Further proofs of the extent to which the revival spirit has taken hold of Treorky and its neighbourhood have been furnished me by many who have not only attended Mr. Evan Roberts's successful meetings, but who have witnessed the remarkable progress of spiritual work which has marked the past few months. The great gatherings at Bethlehem to-day, at Cwmpark Baptist Chapel in the morning, and simultaneously at Bethania, and the extraordinary prayer meetings held nightly at Noddfa, indicate the intense earnestness which prevails, for all are not only well attended, but conducted with an energy which betokens the presence of real, active spiritual life. And before entering into an account of the meetings which I attended to-day, a few words must be said about the effects of the revival upon the community, for the effect is very apparent in many directions.

Perhaps the most prominent feature is the lessening of drunkenness, for the night marches of praying and singing converts seem to have induced a considerable number of well-known drunkards to abandon their evil ways, and, in some instances, to identify themselves with the religious movement. Instances of the "toning down" of the language of underground hauliers have been occasionally referred to, but a colliery official told me to-day that he had quietly and unseen, watched a haulier, while walking toward the pit bottom, turn aside more than once, and when at last he came up to him found him praying fervently for forgiveness of the sins of his life and he had been a somewhat notorious young fellow.

In another instance I heard of a "banks-man" who continually talks to his fellow workers at the pit top about religious matters, and of groups of three or four men praying together in their working-places. But, perhaps, the most striking case is that of a "master-haulier," who takes such a prominent part in the prayer meetings at Noddfa, Treorky. He was at one time, the captain of the local football team, and in one of his public prayers he said the Lord knew that those who formerly took the leading part in football now led in the tug-of-war team for Jesus Christ. He is most inspiring, and takes part in these meetings every night. In one of his prayers he earnestly asked the Lord "to come with us to the Cardiff-square meeting" (meaning the open-air meeting in-the square near the Cardiff Arms Hotel).

As indicating the influence which this movement has had upon the "football craze" in the neighbourhood, it is said that there is in Noddfa Sunday School a "football class" comprised almost entirely of ex-footballers. A prominent colliery official connected with the Rhondda and Treharris, speaking in a revival meeting at Ton Pentre, spoke highly of the noble work done by the "Western Mail" in connection with the revival move and said he hoped the day would come when they would publish a prayer meeting edition instead of a football edition. Last week the Rev. B. W. Davies, Ton, publicly announced that among the people who had come into his chapel (Hebron) was a man who had handed him what he called his "bona-fide club" ticket.

The colliery managers in many places can tell some interesting stories about the effects of the revival upon the workmen. Mr. D. A. Thomas, M.P., informs me that the manager of the colliery in which he is interested tells him that the revival had made them better colliers, and I have heard similar remarks made by other colliery officials, the clearest indication of the effects of the revival being greater regularity in the attendance of the men at work.

Perhaps, however, the most direct case of the influence of Mr. Evan Roberts's pithy remarks is that of a Cilfynydd collier who was "cropped," or threatened, for "filling dirty coal." He told the officials that he would "make them sit up for it," because he would get the works committee to take it up with the Miners' Federation. Instead of going to the committee, he went to hear Evan Roberts, who talked about the Spirit in a man's heart making it impossible for him to do a mean action, and the result was he went back to the colliery office, and asked to be allowed to work on, that he did not intend bringing anything before the works committee, and that he would never again give cause of complaint about "dirty coal" being filled into his trams. Needless to say, his offer was promptly accepted.

Surely, a revival which does these things must be good for the community generally.

Chapter 19 - An idle Sipendiary

TREORKY, Thursday, December 1.

From a merely spectacular point of view, apart from its warmth, intelligence, and spiritual fervour, the great meeting held in Noddfa Baptist Chapel, Treorky, this evening was the most remarkable I have yet attended in connection with Mr. Evan Roberts's progress through the mining districts in connection with the Welsh revival. There is ordinary sitting accommodation for upwards of 1,500 people in the building, and it has often accommodated 2,000, yet it was manifest about an hour before the time fixed for opening the evening Service that on this occasion it would be totally inadequate to meet the needs of the vast crowds who were flocking its precincts. The danger of a "rush" was so great that arrangements were made to provide for the safety of the people. When the congregation was in its place the sight from the rostrum was a magnificent one as one looked at the tiers of people on the galleries which surround the entire chapel, while the body of the immense structure was simply packed.

But the day's work had been begun at Blaencwm with singular fervour, the pro's being very impressive, and the converts names being called out faster than they could be taken down, while the "testi" were hurled out to such an extent as to interfere occasionally with the practical work of filling in the "saved list" With this preparation and the manifest "fire" already existing at Treorky, no wonder the night gathering was of a deeply moving character.

By the bye, there is plenty of scope still in the Rhondda for any and every effort that may be put forth, for, although Sir Marchant Williams states that the result of the revival in the district over which he presides as stipendiary magistrate has been to reduce drunkenness to such an extent as to leave him practically nothing todo with such matters. I regret that hitherto the effect upon the work of the magistrates in the Rhondda is not appreciable. The "drunken" cases were heavy at Ystrad on Monday, and there was no marked difference at Porth to-day. Still, the police in the upper part of the Rhondda, as elsewhere, foresee the probability of much good being done. Both in the upper part of the Rhondda and in Pontypridd some of the police themselves men of high repute in every sense quietly identify themselves with the movement, some of the converts being in the force. But the number of converts hitherto made in the Rhondda, large as it is, is as yet not so great in proportion to the population as it was in the Trecynon, Mountain Ash, Aberand Ynysbwl districts (swept by the revival)all in Sir Marchant Williams's stipendiary district; and the direct results in police-court records are, therefore, yet to come.

In the collieries the best attendance at present is in the portion of the district furthest away from the centres visited by Mr. Evan Roberts. Why? Well, because this week is less regular than usual, the men in hundreds of cases keeping away in order to attend the revival meetings. But there are hopes of better attendance in future, because as I was informed by an Ocean Colliery official to-day, a considerable number of "regular boozers" have joined the Churches, and there is a decided diminution, in the consumption of intoxicants. As bearing, upon another aspect of the effects of the revival. I may mention that Mr. Middleton, manager of the Park Colliery. Cwmpark, states that he has only heard one oath in his colliery during the week, whereas previous to the starting of this religious revival in the district he used to hear hundreds, if not thousands, daily. He points to the quiet demeanour of the workmen. In this he confirms the version given, by other officials, who, however, described the condition of things somewhat differently. "There is no cheek," said one. "There is a good deal of singing, underground and above ground," said another. "Hymns instead of comic songs," added still another.

But to return to the great night meeting. Passing into the immense building through the crowd which surrounded the chapel, Mr. Evan Roberts was so impressed with the scene that he immediately asked for prayers for a blessing on those who were outside, as well as those who had gained admittance. Thin was instantly responded to, and the young revivalist next called for prayers for a young man who had, not consented to come to Christ while he (the speaker) was on his way into that meeting. It was a sister's request, he said, and if they prayed that the man would be saved before dawn he would be. He was certain of it, for the Bible told them to expect such answers to their petitions. What they needed was not only to get the world to believe, but to get the Church to believe. He was confident that they were going to have souls saved at the afternoon meeting, and they came35 of them. But there was not an atom of credit due to man, to any man, it was simply, due to the Holy Ghost. The principal subject of the evening's address was "Faith."

Chapter 20 - Unexpected Features

PENTRE, Friday, December 2.

There was a change in the programme of the revival meetings to-day, and the interest was, if any-thing, heightened by the absence from Pentre of Mr. Evan Roberts in the afternoon. In order, presumably, to give the young evangelist a little rest, it had been decided that the Pentre meetings should not begin until Friday evening, and it was only very late on Thursday night it was announced that there would be an afternoon prayer meeting at one of the chapels. But the people of the district, calculating upon the unceasing continuance of the gatherings had come in crowds, many from a distance in the morning, and were turned away. Mr. Evan Roberts, taking advantage of the occasion, left for Llantrisant, in order to put in an appearance with the young ladies who have for some days been carrying on a mission there, and on his return he looked stall eager for work.

The evening meeting at Moriah Chapel had been announced for six p.m., and long before that time the building was full, although it was known that Mr. Evan Roberts would not be there for some time, If at all. The first of the revivalists to come in was Miss Rees, of Loughor, the young lady whose story of her visit to the gipsy encampment thrilled the Trecynon meeting about a. fortnight ago. She took her seat, alone, in the "big pew," and presently began to sing some of the beautifully touching hymns of the revival. After the congregation had joined her she opened the meeting with prayer, and afterwards spoke alternately in Welsh and English, taking practically charge of the proceedings, as there was at first, a seeming lack of readiness on the part of individuals in the congregation to take part. Gradual]y, however, the reserve broke down, and prayer after prayer, "testimony," exhortation, and hymn came with a promptitude and enthusiasm which was refreshing for a first meeting. Miss Mary Davies (Gorseinon) and Miss Annie Davies (Maesteg) came, and the solo-singing became more and mere touching so that the crowded congregation could not help being imbued with the spirit which everywhere prevails, while the mere state of curiosity to see Mr. Evan Roberts has been overcome. The most eloquent and fervent in prayer, certainly, were the women of the congregation, and the number who spoke and prayed here was larger than at any of the previous meetings.

There was also another feature which I had not expected to find at Pentre, viz., more English in the speaking, the praying, and the singing. Another was the state of things when, at half-past seven o'clock, Mr. Evan Roberts arrived. Then there was a general hush of expectation, soon broken by an 'enthusiastic outburst of

"Pen Calfaria,
Nac aed hwnw byth o'm cof."

The revivalist was in a cheerful, aggressively cheerful or, should I say, cheerfully aggressive mood. He took the "Diolch iddo" of one of the verses of the hymn sung as a kind of text, and dwelt upon the necessity for unstinted, active, cheerful gratitude to God. He compared the state of the heathen with the state of Wales, and pictured in forcible words the surprise which he felt at the fact that so many in Wales rejected the Love of Christ. Practically applying this to the business of every-day life, the speaker dwelt upon the advantages, even from a temporal point of view, of absolute faith in God. It was not until the Church itself was fully imbued with faith that the pagan would receive the blessings of the Word. Many who sang, "Iesu, Iesu, 'rwyt ti'n ddigon" ("Jesus, Jesus, all-sufficient") could not possibly believe what they were singing, or they would not go to the places which they frequented. They were, therefore, hypocritical in singing it.

Suddenly a voice from the rostrum breaks in with music, and the congregation begin singing,

"Duw mawr o rhyfeddodau maith,"

and the rolling basses are heard as they have been heard at so many places. But Mr. Evan Roberts is not satisfied. He actually tells the people that they lack the spirit of gratitude. They had, he said, been fervent and spirited in their appeal for his presence, whereas now they sang a triumphant song of praise as if they were half-hearted, Of course, there was a second rendering of the hymn, with much more life and energy in it, and the revivalist took up the thread of his discourse as if nothing had happened. But he had not spoken long before there came an interruption from the front of the gallery a young lady singing, to the tune of "The Last Rose of Summer," the words of the hymn,

"Dyma Feibl anwyl Iesu."

A rendering made popular by Miss Annie Davies.

However, as the interruptions to Mr. Roberts's speech had come, so did the interruptions come even to the work of reciting verses and giving testimonies. The congregation on this particular night seemed to be full of singing, but it was noticeable that it was very fine and fervent singing, tenderer than has been the case in any other place. The hymn "O, yr Oen, yr addfwyn Oen," -was sung with thrilling effect, and even though it interrupted a peculiarly impressive portion of the service, the young revivalist simply clapped his hands and cried out "Ardderchog."

During one portion of the proceedings come of the people in the congregation cried "Hush!" when more than one spoke at a time or when a singer interrupted Mr. Roberts himself, whereupon Mr. Roberts said he hoped they would not indulge in any such interruptions as crying "hush" to anybody. If a drunken man had come forward to sing or say anything he would not have interested him, because, in his experience, he had known a drunken man coming in to a service and yet being saved within a quarter of an hour, for the Spirit sobered even a drunken man. "Therefore," he said, "in any case don't say 'Hush' to anyone."

Chapter 21 - Enthusiasm at Pentre

PENTRE, Sunday, December 4.

Crowded with incidents and crowned with success is a phrase that may very well be applied to the visit of Mr. Evan Roberts and his band of evangelists to Pentre, for there were stirring events on Saturday and to-day. The meeting at Silolh Congregational Chapel on Saturday afternoon was largely attended even at the outset, although operations at the neighbouring collieries had not ceased. When I entered the chapel shortly after two o'clock, Mr. Roberts was not there the lady evangelists had not arrived and yet there seemed to be in the atmosphere that indefinable "some" which invariably betokens fervency before a word had been spoken. Presently a ministerial visitor rises in the "big pew," and said this year had been a wonderful year wonderful in many respects. He referred to the Russo-Japanese War and other matters, and added that not the least wonderful was this religious revival in Wales. The news of the success of this new crusade was wonderful. While he was speaking Mr. Evan Roberts walked in, and a woman in the body of the chapel recited, as a fit complement to the minister's few words, the Welsh hymn:

"Newyddion braf a ddaeth i'n bro,
Hwy haeddant gael eu dwyn ar go,
Enillodd Iesu mawr y dydd,
Caiff carcharorion fyn'd yn rhydd"

This is usually sung to the tune "Ernan," but here it was sung to "Luther's Hymn," as soon as the last notes died away, another single voice in the distance started "'Dyma gariad fel y moroedd," and, alter this, from a rev. gentleman who sat on the pulpit stairs, came the first three words or Cardinal Newman's "Lead, kindly Light," and the congregation very sweetly joined in rendering the hymn to Purday's tune, "Standon," which is the only one heard at these gatherings. Then there came the voice of a workman, engaged in earnest and really eloquent prayer in Welsh, suppli-cating the blessings of the Spirit on that gathering, and, in rhythmical cadences, recounting the "saving" scenes witnessed elsewhere. They had for years, he said, been praying for an outpouring of the Spirit, and it had come upon the Churches. "Yr ydym wedi gweled gwaethaf Satan lawer gwaith," he declared, "ond nid ydym wedi gweled goreu Crist hyd yn awr" ("We have seen Satan's worst many times, but have never seen Christ's best until now").

Mr. Evan Roberts, ascending the pulpit, exclaimed, "You need not ask God to send the Spirit to this meeting, friends; the Spirit is here. Pray that you may be baptised with it"

A young woman, sitting under the shadow of the balcony, rose, and in passionate tones, but in a voice evidently almost lost by recent straining, proclaimed:

"I do believe, I will believe,
That Jesus died for me."

The young revivalist smilingly remarked, "She has lost her voice in telling the people about her Saviour."

While the great congregation sang the well-known hymn, I inquired who the lady was, and was informed that she hailed from Trewhere, during the past nine or ten days, full of the revival "fire," she had been so active that she alone had brought no fewer than 105 converts to the local churches.

When the singing was finished, Mr. Evan Roberts resumed, pointing out that the object in view in praying now was, not so much to "achub" (save), as "Plygu yr Egliwys" (Bend the Church). Our belief in the Churches was a stumbling block. It was not open unbelief, but half-belief, and there must be no such stumbling-block. Just as Achan was cast out of the camp of old, so must any and every Achan be cast out of Christ's Church now. But he maintained that all that was necessary was to get the Churches to realise thoroughly and absolutely the love of Christ. While he was speaking, there arose from the "big pew" the voice of Miss Annie Davies, Maestag, bursting forth into song

"Wrth gofio'i ruddfanau'n yr Ardd
A'i chwys yn ddefnynau o waed,
Aredig ar gefn oedd mor hardd,
A'i daro a chleddyf ei Dad;
Ei' arwain i Galfari fryn,
A'i hoelio ar groesbren o'i foddd,

Pa dafod all dewi am hyn?
Pa galon mor galed na thodd?"

It is often sung to the tune "St. Andrew's," but Miss Davies had found a tune more suitable to her purpose from a slow, impressive, appealing solo, but I was unable to ascertain the title of it, for scarcely had silence come upon the touched congregation before the young lady from Treherbert already alluded to, was again on her feet, and, with her face glowing with fervour, she exclaimed:

Count your blessings, count them one by one,
Count your blessings, see what God hath done;
Count your blessings, name them one by one,
And it will surprise you what the Lord, hath done.

This was instantly struck up by Miss A.M. Rees, of Gorseinon, one of the evangelists; who sang very effectively, the congregation, after a while, joining in very heartily. Then on subsequent "rereats," Miss Rees varied the last line into "Go and tell the people what the Lord hath done."

This "caught on" immensely, as it seemed to suit the spirit of the meeting admirably. Just a few words of prayer for the saving of souls, and someone struck up "Throw out the life" which was sung by the congregation with some warmth, but it was not energetic enough for Mr. Roberts. He got up and asked if they had actually seen men saving life at sea. If not, let them try to realise what "throwing out the life-line" meant, and they would sing it with a power which was now lacking. It was, he said, one of the lessons of the revival to show that they really were anxious to save souls. One notable feature of this gathering was the change in the character of the hymns, for although different tunes are sung to the same hymns, varying generally according to the denomination that predominates in the particular congregation, there has not hitherto been such a series of departures from what has been regarded as the most popular hymns. "O na bawn i fel Efe" may be taken as an instance, as well as those already quoted in Welsh and English.

While Mr. Evan Roberts was speaking on implicit obedience to the Spirit, and summarising the point into four words, "You must do anything and everything, anywhere and everywhere" (which he repeated in English), there was a stir in the aisle, and three young people marched towards the "big pew." Down from the pulpit came the evangelist and, extending his hand to welcome the newcomers, he said, "This is Sidney Evans and two other workers," and within a few minutes the newcomers were at work.

Mr. Sidney Evans ascended the pulpit, and with the familiarity of a brother Mr. Roberts turned to him and said, "A oes genyt ti air i'w ddweyd wrth y bobl?" ("Hast thou a word to say to the people?"). Replying with a smile, Mr. Evans (whose boyish appearance was very striking) said he had come there to receive, and in a few pithy sentences he dwelt upon the fulness with which God could endow people who came ready to receive. He declared that upwards of 300 people had been converted - at Morriston since last Sunday. Then, taking up his theme, he said, "God has a blessing for every one who asks. He does not throw His blessings as a father sometimes throws nuts for his children to scramble for it is a blessing for each one."

When the recital of testimonies came the scenes witnessed became very impressive, and in the course of the proceedings a number of converts were enrolled, one young man remaining obdurate, though under deep emotion, until the meeting had actually been closed. In the last group he was spoken to by Mr. Roberts, and was added to the "saved list."

It may be added that among the workers who arrived during the meeting were Mr. Evan Roberts's young sister, seemingly only fifteen or sixteen years of age, but full of the work, and Miss Hopkins, of Loughor. The two subsequently proceeded to Tonypandy to assist in a meeting that evening, Miss Williams, of Gorseinon, joining the others at Ton.

The evening meeting was an extraordinary one altogether. Jerusalem Chapel was simply crowded and overcrowded body of chapel, aisles, galleries, lobby, staircases, big seat, pulpit,and outside stood a seething mass of people waiting for possible chances of getting in, Hebron Chapel, only a stone's-throw away, was also full; so was the Congregational Chapel.

When I had managed to work my way slowly and with considerable difficulty into Jerusalem Chapel the first disfeatures I caught were those of the radiant missioner, Mr. M'Taggart, whose abandonment of his Anglican Catholic position in order to "work for Christ and for souls" I have previously mentioned. He sat in a deacon's chair just under the pulpit, and presently, when invited by Mr. Roberts, he spoke a few sentences in English, crisp, trite sayings, which were thoroughly appreciated even by the Welsh section. He also told his hearers that his adopted son had reached there that night, having walked all the way from London in order to receive some of the blessings of the Welsh revival,

When he was describing the picture which he was trying to impress upon his hearers Miss Annie Davies, Maesteg, broke in with

"Wrth gofio'i ruddfanau'n yr Ardd,"

and when she had concluded Mr. Roberts proceeded, but had not gone far before she again, evidently under very deep emotion, began singing,

"Dim ond Iesu" ("Jesus only"),

when she utterly broke down, and, sobbing aloud, exclaimed, "0! Iesu, Iesu, drosof fi" ("O! Jesus, Jesus, for me!") She wept bitterly, and caused hundreds to sob, raising her voice in loud lamentation. The tension became painful, overcoming the revivalist himself, and the position was only relieved by the chapel presenter striking up.

"Pen Calfaria,
Pen Calfaria,
Nac aed hwnw byth o'n cof,"

and it was sung by the congregation with pathos as well as fervour. Miss Annie Davies, whose voice has been to some extent strained by the work of the past fortnight, was unable to take any part in the service afterwards. Mr. Roberts, however, spoke at some length, and the scene when "testi" were called for was a very remarkable one. Miss May John sang with splendid effect the Welsh rendering of "Oh happy day," viz,

"O, hapus awr, hapus awr,
Maddeuodd Iesu 'meiau mawr,"

and the refrain was taken up with unenthusiasm by the vast congregation. Presently the strange mixture of impromptus which often comes with the hymn "Come to Jesus just now," was, if possible, extended here. The names of converts were being enrolled, and there was an extraordinary number of them. They were shouted from all parts of the building, and great enthusiasm was aroused. "Dyma Nefoedd" ("Here is Heaven"), exclaimed Mr. Evan Roberts, and Miss May John from the front of the gallery took it for a cue, sing as she clapped her hands

"Dyma Nefoedd, dyma Nefoedd,
Dyma Nefoedd, 'r awr hon;'
R awr hon, dyma Nefoedd
Dyma Nefoedd 'r awr hon."

and the new verse rang through the building with a note of triumph that must have reverberated from the open windows through the street and along the hillsides.

An old lady, with snow-white hair, got up in the congregation, and, after thanking God for the privilege of being present and wishing that she could have enjoyed the many blessings which the Welsh friends enjoyed, she asked if it was not possible to have a few words from Mr. Roberts in the English language. But in any event, she added, she rejoiced to see that great meeting and to see the great work that was being done.

Mr. Roberts replied in the English language that they would do the best they could, but the time was very short, and they were anxious to save souls. It turned out that the lady in question was Mrs. Anderson, of Margate, sister to the editor of a London paper. Afterwards she privately confirmed what she had said about the joy she felt, and hoped the work would go on increasing.

After the results of the night meeting, from the point of view of the enrolment of converts, I was not surprised to be informed that no fewer than 55 converts had declared themselves.

Notwithstanding the steady downpour of rain at Pentre on Sunday, the various chapels were literally besieged, crowds of people waiting for hours outside in the cold and damp in the hope of being eventually able to gain admission, hundreds having to wait in vain.

Chapter 22 - In Fresh Fields

CEARPHILLY, Monday, December 5.

Coming from the midst of the huge population of the large centre of the Rhondda Valleys to Caerphilly, Mr. Evan Robert and the singing evangelists have met with an equally responsive spirit. They have been met by crowds for whose accommodation the chapels are totally inadequate, and the revival meetings remind one of the stories of the old revival, in connection with which the people of the country flocked to the centre from large tracts of country. To see the Market square of Caerphilly thronged, while two or three chapels were crowded to overflowing, under such circumstances, was a sight in itself worth seeing, for it indicates the hold which the religious revival has taken of the people in the town. There was a service at the Welsh Methodist Chapel in the morning, and, though the evangelist had not attended, there was a very interesting gathering. Farmers on horseback, tradesmen in traps, hundreds by motor-cars, hundreds more by train, colliers and other workmen trudging on foot; there was a variety presented, and still it was, as might have been anticipated, a quiet, pleasant throng, evidently bent on seeing and hearing the revival and the man, I say the man, advisedly, for nowhere else have I seen anything like the rush of people in the street just to catch a glimpse of Mr. Evan Roberts when, he merely passed from the chapel to the chapel-keeper's house at the close of the afternoon service.

The afternoon service was held in the Calvinistic Methodist Chapel, and the congregation was so closely packed that the people actually trod on the gas pipes, jambing them to such an extent as to make it impossible to get light to hold the evening meeting there. Still, under the difficulties presented by the overcrowded state of the building, the work was carried out with enthusiasm. Mr. Roberts was accompanied by three of the young lady evangelists. Miss Rees (Gorseinon), Miss Mary Davies (Gorseinon), and Miss Annie Davies (Maesteg). The outstanding feature of the service was a, passionately fervent prayer of a young woman whose appeals for her father, sister, and little brother were not only pathetic, but whose whole prayer, for eloquence and "wrestling with the Spirit" was, perhaps, more touching than any public prayer that has been heard since the advent of the revivalist in the mining districts of the upper part of Glamorgan. There was hymn-singing in the course of the service, and some of the congregation sang during a portion of this prayer, but the very fervency and "inspira" of the supplication seemed to carry everything before it, and even the music of this "singing revival" gave way to the powerful and pathetic prayer. The solo-singing, always effective, was for once lost, sight of an indication that the second stage of the revival is being reached. It will be remembered that at one of the services last Week Mr. Roberts said that some people objected to so much singing, "but," he explained, "there are two stages of a revival; singing first and praying afterwards. The second stage will come."

The Van-road chapel was crowded before six p.m. for a service supposed to begin at seven. There was no wasted time,however, for the congregation sang Welsh and English hymns alternately, so that by the appointed hour the meeting had attained a high pitch of enthusiasm and fervour.

Mr. Evan Roberts arrived about a quarter to seven, and promptly rose to address the congregation, and, notwithstanding the crowded state of the aisles and lobby, it is significant that there was absolute silence while he spoke, and that his queries, put with a view of setting people thinking quite as much as eliciting answers, were replied to with intelligence and quickness as well as reverence. The heat was intense, and the atmosphere close, so that Mr. Roberts had, to appeal for more ventilation, and while the congregation was slacking its "crush" over the staircase which led up from the vestry he asked the people to sing "Lead, kindly Light," and to do it prayerfully. The hymn was sung in English, very deliberately, and seemingly with full responsibility of the serious request made to them.

On resuming his remarks Mr. Roberts said he had been compelled to say that he believed that this revival would not only come to Wales, and reach all Wales, but that it would go over England, Scotland, and Ireland as well. More than that, he considered that we were on the eve of a revival which would go over the whole world. They were told that in the last days certain things would happen, and he read his Bible to mean that we lived in the "last days." Young men "saw visions," and others "dreamed dreams" there was bloodshed on earth and there were signs in the heavens. He had, he said, himself seen a vision of a candle burning brightly, and then the light of the sun shining upon all; and he took it to mean the light of the Gospel first as a, candle, and then the great sun shining upon the whole world.

When "public confession" is invited, the responses are fairly numerous, but it is a new "family" unused to the orderly disorder of the revival, and the question "Will everyone who confess Christ rise" only brings a few, say 40 or 50 people, to their feet. Bringing his hand down somewhat heavily upon the big pulpit Bible, Mr. Evan Roberts, raising his voice in surprise, ask, "What! Is this the number of these in this congregation who confess Jesus Christ?" The Rev. Tawelfryn Thomas, standing on the temporary platform beside the revivalist, shouts out "No, no!" and the audience realise that they have not come to an entertainment, but to "show their side" and the response came, as might have been expected.

The responses did not even then become so numerous proportionately to the size of the congregation as might have been anticipated if the meeting had been packed by members of Churches of the various denominations. What was the secret? Well, simply that among those who were present there were very many persons who were not members anywhere. In this respect the meeting answered its purpose much better than many of the gatherings which have been held elsewhere. "Throw out the life-line" was sung, and the converts enrolled were numerous, The chapel is supposed to accommodate about 500 people. Admit, if you like, that, packed as it was, it held 650 that night, Then just look at the proportion. Thirty to thirty-five converts declaring for Christ, and others getting up gradually as the service went on until the number had reached fifty-nine! It was interesting work, and the singing of "Diolch iddo," "For you I am praying," Come to Jesus just now," and other hymns went on, prayers alternating with exhortation and praise until a little after one o'clock in the morning, when Mr. Evan Roberts, in order to get ready for Tuesday's work, left the meeting to go to his lodgings. The meeting was still carried on, the Rev. T. Bush, the Rev. C. Tawelfryn Thomas, and others taking part, and by about four o'clock in the morning for the people did not seem to want to go away the list of converts had run up to ninety and nine!

Tuesday, December 6.

Notwithstanding the rain and the knowledge that the chapels were far too small to accommodate any great numbers, the crowds who came to Caerphilly to bear and see, or try to hear and see, Mr. Evan Roberts to-day were just as large as they were on the previous day. The sights in the open-air were not so manifest to the casual observer, perhaps, because, instead of being brought together into the square near the "Twyn" Chapel. the people were scattered about, the meetings being held in various chapels at the other end of the town, and there was, fortunately, some uncertainty as to where the missioner would speak, or whether he would deliver addresses at more than one place of worship.

The afternoon meeting was at Bethel Congregational Chapel. I may at once say that this gathering was much more like the Rhondda gatherings than the previous night's service had been. Mr. Evan Roberts spoke at some length, dealing specially with the condition of Wales. He said it pained him to think of how many people in the Principality lived careless lives; how many lived drunken and sinful lives, and, oh, how many frequently cursed and swore and used the sacred names of God and Jesus Christ in vain! When he pondered over that terrible fact he dreaded the sight which the Judgment Day would present!

Two of the meetings were not concluded till the early hours of Wednesday morning. One of the converts was the man who declared the previous night that there was an incident in his history which prevented him from making his confession. A man and wife, having left one of the meetings in the evening, returned in their slippers, after having been to rest, and became converted. It was estimated that on Tuesday night at all the chapels there must have been over 123 converts.

Chapter 23 - "Fire" at Senghenydd

SENGHENYDD, Wednesday, December 7.

The arrival of Mr. Evan Roberts at Senghenydd to-day was hailed with joy by large numbers of people.

There was before half-past one in the afternoon a crowded congregation in the Calvinistic Methodist, Chapel, and the hymn-singing mainly in Welsh here, was very effective. A hymn that I have not heard at any of the previous meetings was sung here:

"Cof am y cyfiawn Iesu,
Y Person mwyaf hardd,
Ar noswaith oer anesmwyth,
Yn chwysu yn yr Ardd;
A'r eliwys yn ddafnau cochion,
Yn llifo tua'r llawr
Bydd canu am ei gariad
I dragwyddoldeb mawr."

This was sung to the old tune "Penry," and. repeated with emphatic heartiness. A young lady from Bedwas rose in the gallery and, in English, said she had gone to Mr. Evan Roberts on the previous night to ask him pray for her. "What do you, want?" he asked, and she replied that she did not think she was doing enough for Jesus Christ. Ultimately, he advised her to tell her neighbours in Bedwas, and others, about her Saviour. She went home, and in the morning when in the train she spoke to a woman from Pentre, Rhondda Valley, who said neither she nor her husband went to any chapel, although some of the children went. She prayed with the woman, but at first without avail. She prayed again, and the woman accepted Christ, and then promised to try to influence her husband. Then the young lady added, "I hope my brother is in this congregation. Will you pray for him?" Several prayers were offered, and ten minutes or a quarter of an hour later a shout was raised from the far end of the gallery. Her brother was converted, and there was a mighty shout of "Diolch iddo" and "Songs of Praise I will ever give to Thee."

But perhaps the most peculiar instance of her work which she now gave was that of a young man who did not know how to break off an engagement for a championship fight. She was going to pray for him, and, as there was yet time during the week, she would go to work, and she believed she would succeed.

An elderly man in the gallery got up and declared that He was one of the 63 converts of the previous night. He had, he said, been a backslider, and rejoiced that he had been brought to see the seriousness of his position. He earnestly appealed for prayers for himself and others of the same kind who required strength to keep steadfast.

Meanwhile, Mr. Evan Roberts, accompanied by Miss Mary Davies (Gorseinon), Miss Annie Davies (Maesteg), and Mr. M'Taggart, had gone to the Welsh Baptist Chapel, where there was a somewhat smaller congregation, and where the meeting was, for a time, decidedly colder, so cold, indeed, as to affect the young revivalist with deep emotion. He prayed and asked others to pray for a downpour of the Spirit, and presently there was a warmer feeling, the responses to the invitatation to "confess" being numerous.

Among those who spoke from the gallery was one of the converts, who had come to the meeting at Caerphilly after prayers had been specially offered for him, and he now publicly referred to his own and his father's conversion. He also made special reference to the conversion of some of his "pals," one of them a somewhat noted pugilist, and hoped that another whom he and other friends had been trying to get to join them in turning over a new leaf would now be won over. He appealed very forcibly to young men in the congregation to listen to the appeals that were being made to them, and not to waste their time any longer in idle pursuits.

"Throw out the life-line" was sung with great earnestness, and in this context I may be allowed to introduce a really useful Welsh translation of that popular hymn

"Teflwch raff Bywyd dros war y don ddu,
Mae aew frawd yn rhyferthwy y Ili;
Mae'n frawd i rywunpwy feiddia yn awr
Daflu rhaff Bywyd i'r perygl mawr?
Teflwch raff Bywyd,
Teflwch raff Bywyd,

Mae rhywun yn myned i'w fedd;
Teflwch raff Bywyd,
Teflwch raff Bywyd
Mae rhywun yn suddo'n ddihedd."

Written on a "papyr bach" (checkweight ticket) of a colliery worker, this translation was handed to me by Mr. J. T. Williams, of Rhymney, who stated that it is the work of Mr. Daniel Davies, a deacon with the Calvinistic Methodists at that place. I think, it will "take" well at the meetings, and commend it as a useful addition to the repertoire of those who so spontaneously strike up the hymns which send such a glow through the hearts and the countenances of the Welsh section at these meetings.

Chapter 24 - The Rhondda Re-visited

RHONDDA, Thursday, December 8.

The return of Mr. Evan Roberts to the Rhondda Valleys had been looked forward to with considerable interest by the people of Ferndale and the Rhondda Fach generally. When it was announced that Mr. Evan Roberts and the lady evangelists had not arrived in Ferndale on Thursday afternoon there was some disappointment felt, but there was a crowded congregation in Trerhondda Chapel at two o'clock in the afternoon and the usual revival meeting was proceeded with, the hymn-singing, addresses, and prayers being particularly fervent and earnest. Amongst the speakers during the afternoon was Mrs. Baxter, wife of the editor of a London religious paper, who said that she had for 46 years endeavoured to work for Christ's Kingdom, and she was glad to see this great revival going on in Wales. "Diolch iddo," she said, and many in the congregation shouted "Amen."

Some of the colliers of Ferndale and Mardy were very enthusiastic in their exclamations and in their prayers, several of them laying special emphasis upon the work which was being done in making men sober. One of them said that a little more than six months ago he himself was singing in a public-house to amuse people, but he now sang songs of praise to God, and was more earnest to-day than on the day of his conversion. He laid special emphasis upon the necessity for workmen who were professing Christians to be circumspect and upright in their conduct lest the lads who worked with them should emulate their bad examples.

About a quarter to five o'clock. Mr. Evan Roberts arrived by train at Fendale, accompanied by Miss A. M. Rees (Gorseinon), Miss Mary Davies (Gorseinon), and Miss Annie Davies (Maesteg).

Trerhondda Chapel was well filled before six o'clock for a, meeting announced to comat seven, and although overflow meetings were announced to be held at Tabernacle Chapel, the Welsh Wesleyan Chapel, and with the English Presbyterians and at the higher Grade School, the congregation continued to grow until the precincts of the chapel and the vestry had been filled, while a crowd stood patiently waiting in the street outside the gates.

Mr. Evan Roberts arrived at the meeting about a quarter to seven and found it warm and enthusiastic. He proceeded to deliver an address in Welsh, in the course of which he dwelt upon the imperative necessity of awakening the churches to the realisation of the greatness of God's works and the love of Christ. While he was dwelling upon the beauties of God's work as seen in Nature the vast congregation burst out into the rousing hymn, "Duw mawr y rhyfeddodan maith," which was repeated again and again. Then, proceeding, he said that there was no middle place between Heaven and hell, and it was as well for everybody to realise it, whereupon a voice was heard crying out, "Here is one for Heaven at any rate," and another enthusiastic member of the congregation shouted out, "Any passengers for Mynydd Seion!" a quaint way of inviting converts.

"I have come 200 miles to confess that I love Christ," said one, "and I have come a great distance to enjoy what you are getting," said another. "I need Thee every hour," was sung in Welsh. One speaker said what was necessary was, as Mr. Evan Roberts had told them, to pray to save the congregations and to awaken the Churches. Another speaker referred with joy to the news he had received of public-houses being emptied at Kilgerran. A young lady from Ferndale got into the pulpit and said, "They have asked, me to sing. I don't understand much music, but Christ may sing through me," and she sang very sweetly "Tyr'd ato, bechadur." This meeting continued until a late hour, and was carried on with the utmost enthusiasm.

Simultaneously with the proceedings described, another remarkable meeting was being held in the Higher Grade School, where Miss A. M. Roes, of Gorseinon, conducted an English service. At the outset, as no one seemed to take the initiative, Miss Rees rose and said that at the revival meetings it was not usually necessary to ask anybody to take part, even to the extent of giving out a hymn, for when the Spirit moved them the people were only too ready to take part, and she hoped that no one at this gathering would for a moment quench the Spirit in their own hearts or in those of others. A hymn was given out by a gentleman in the congregation, which was taken up very energetically by all.

Then occurred one of those remarkable incident which now and again mark the proceedings in connection with this strange revival. A young man rose in the middle of the congregation, and said he had come all the way from Caerphilly to give his testimony. He could not be quiet, although his past conduct, to which he was about to refer, was such as made him feel heartily ashamed of himself. He was one of those who had been referred to as one of the converts at Caerphilly. He was a member of the Caerphllly Football Club, and he regretted to have to say it,he not only played football, but wherever he went, in the train or otherwise, he used to take with him in his pocket a pack of cards, with which he used to gamble, frequently losing money which he ought to have given- to his poor mother. He used to take about with him in his pocket also bottles of whisky, young though he was, and last Christmas, between the cards and the whisky, he lost 26 shillings, and there was his poor mother in the house, and he broke down sobbing, and could not comprehend his narrative. The congregation fervently sang "Diolch iddo, byth am gofio llwch y llawr," and "Songs of Praises," Miss May John, R.A.M., taking the leading part in the singing. Resuming his narrative, the young man said that last Monday night he was for three-quarters of an hour wrestling with the devil, but ultimately he found salvation, and hoped to be able to devote his energies to the work of telling young men of his own age all he could about the love of the Saviour. He said that after his conversion he handed to Miss Rees a dance card, "for," he added, "he had also wasted valuable time in connection with dances."

Miss Rees, in confirmation of this narrative, held up one piece of the card indicated, and said she kept it as a trophy of the young man's victory in giving himself up under the circumstances. The other part of the card, she said, was in the possession of Mr. Evan Roberts. Then Miss May John struck up with enthusiasm,

"O happy day that fixed my choice,
On Thee my Saviour and my God,"

In conclusion the young man referred to asked if there were any young fellows like himself in that meeting who had been foolish enough to do what he had used to. If so, he hoped they would do what he had now done, for he certainly could tell them that, this week had been the happiest week in all his life. Miss Rees then left to join Mr. Evan Roberts at the other meeting.

Chapter 25 - Service in a Coal Mine

CWMDARE, Thursday, December 1.

In Ancient Rome Christianity was cradled in persecution and found an asylum in the catacombs. The thought of those secret services, held in a far-off time, came into my mind as I tried to imagine an underground revival service which I was about to attend at the Nantmelyn Colliery, Cwmdare, the property of the Bwllfa and Merthyr Collieries (Limited), whose managing director (Councillor Rees Llewellyn) had given me permission to descend the shaft in order to see the effects of the "revival" underground.

But what a difference to-day. There is no need for secrecy now. Only yesterday there might have been scoffers; to-day there are none. The very atmosphere tingles with a new emotion, and the faith which of old thrived under the persecution of Ancient Rome thrives to-day under the encouragement of all the forces of modern Wales. Scarcely three weeks ago the "Western Mail" held up the lamp of the revival, then burning steadfastly at Loughor. To-day the whole of Wales is ignited. Not alone in sacred buildings and in streets that echo with the pilgrims' hymns, but far down in the bowels of the earth, in the dark coal seams which spread abroad the commercial fame of Wales, a kindlier lamp has been kindled. Christianity calls it the greatest safety lamp that was ever invented for mortal souls.

I went down to the prayer meeting at the Nantmelyn Colliery, 450 feet below the surface, with the manager, Mr. Edward Pugh, a staunch Methodist, for my guide. The workmen on the night shift had gone down half an hour earlier than the usual time so as not to interfere with the operations of the pit. Seventy yards from the bottom of the shaft, in the stables, we came to the prayer meeting. One of the workmen was reading the 6th chapter of St. Matthew to about eighty comrades. He stood erect amongst the group, reading in a dim fantastic light that danced with the swinging lamps and vanished softly into the surrounding darkness. A number of lamps were attached to a heavy post, closely wedged to support the roof, and around the impressive figure the colliers grouped themselves. Some were in the characteristic stooping posture, others half-reclined against the side of the road, with their lamps fastened to their pockets; others,again, stood, in the middle of the passage. Earnest men all of them; faces that bore the sears of the underground toiler; downcast eyes that seemed to be "the homes of silent prayer"; strong frames that quivered with a new emotion.

What must the thoughts of these men have been as the words of the Gospel fell on their ears in this stable transformed into a temple, with the perils of their occupation crowding around them? If the minds of men are moulded by environment, surely they could he subjected to no more impressive experience than this.

Presently the reading of the Scripture stopped, and there came the familiar Welsh hymn

"Gwaith hyfryd iawn a melus yw
Molianu D'enw Di, O! Dduw,
Son am Dy gariad foreu glas,
A'r nos am wirioneddau'th ras."

The hymn must have penetrated through the whole of the workings of the colliery. It echoed along the low roofs and the narrow walls, and when the last echoes were dying away, ever so far off, it seemed a supplicatory voice broke upon our ears. One of the colliers was speaking. "It is not enough to pray," he said, in Welsh, "because if we do not also watch the promises which we make in our prayers will remain unfulfilled. The motto of every true Christian is 'Watch and pray.' Look at that ship which is leaving port. Though she be bound for some definite destination she will never arrive there unless her compass and her helm work in unison. So it is with us. It is easy to cause the roof of a chapel to fall in as the result of prayer; but of what avail is such praying without the necessary watch to walk along the right path?" The speaker went on to refer to attributes of the Christian, and, after alluding to the coldness which prevailed in certain parts of Aberdare towards the revival, he concluded: "In years to come some of us will be sorry to have unheeded the salutary counsels given at the Nantmelyn stable." "Amens'" punctuated the short address, and then the congregation joined in singing the tender verse:

Dyma gyfarfod hyfryd iawn,
Myfi yn llwm a'r Iesu'n llawn;
Myfi yn dlawd, heb feddu dim,
A'r Iesu'n rhoddi pobpeth im.'

Such was the simple service of rugged men: honest, earnest, plain. It was kept up until the moment came for commencing the night's work, and not once, but many times, was God's blessing asked for the honest and proper execution of the work. I stepped into the cage to return, followed by the haunting echoes of the hymn that pleads for a blessing

"Dan dy fendith wrth ymadael
Y dymunem, Arglwydd, fod,
Llona'n calon a Dy gariad,
A'n geneuau a Dy glod;
Dy dangnefedd
Dyro i ni yn barhaus,"

Chapter 26 - Welsh Methodists and the Revivalist, by Rev. Cyndlylan Jones, D.D.

[Reprinted from the "Western Mail," November 19]

I read with amazement an account of a supposed interview with Mr. Evan Roberts. Anyone acquainted with the genius of Welsh Calvinistic Methodism can, without any inquiry, pronounce the insinuations made by the interviewer to the young evangelist not by the evangelist to him to be absolutely baseless, namely, that. the Calvinistic Methodists wish to check the present movement or in any way limit the efforts of the young revivalist. I have this week visited both East and West Glamorgan, and never heard a syllable from any quarter derogatory to the young man or his work, but found everywhere manifestations of great rejoicing that God has at last visited His people. The lust of money and the lust of sport have, for the last few years, been imperilling all that is highest and noblest in our history as a people. The Churches, in their ordinary routine work, have proved themselves powerless to stem the tide of iniquity and to check the revival of barbarism. Now it seems as if the Spirit of God is about to interfere. Thousands of prayers are offered daily that this may prove true.

The young revivalist, like all candidates for the ministry of our Church, is amenable to the presbytery within whose jurisdiction he lives and to the rules and regulations of the connexion at large. But we have provided ample room for men of exceptional intellectual and spiritual endowments, and even if no provision had been made our rules are sufficiently elastic to meet all possible requirements we can always suspend them where they act injuriously on the spiritual life or limit unduly the usefulness of our adherents. The young revivalist need fear no censure or restriction; we view their enthusiasm with gratitude and praise.

Should this movement spread and continue as we pray it will, it is just possible, though not probable, that a, committee will be formed, not to hinder or restrain it, but to help it forward and to give it a new impetus. Should the conditions arise to make this desirable. I may be permitted to express sincere wish that it may be inter-denominational. Let no sectional or local names be mentioned. Who knows but this movement, if properly fostered and encouraged, will burn to the ground the thorny partitions between the several sections of the Church of Christ in Wales? Shall we not labour and pray that it be a national spiritual movement welding all good men and women into one homogeneous community, all aspiring after the same lofty ideals the salvation of souls and the purification of character, private and public? How paltry the explanation in the "Daily Chronicle" interview that the secret of all this great influence is electricity! If it be as described, we mast say, "This is the finger of God."

Before I close permit me to refer to this movement in Ammanford and the attitude of the young poet, the Rev. Nantllals Williams, towards it. Some three years ago I chanced to stay at the house of Mr. William Herbert, of that town, when the latter gave me the narrative of his conversion in Australia. "He told me the story simply as a little child," and I embrace this opportunity of testifying that no book I ever read, no sermon I ever heard, left a deeper mark on my soul. This testimony, remember, comes from one who lived at the heart of the great revival in 1859-60, and went through it, all from beginning to end. The pith of it was the manner he attained to "the fall assurance of the forgiveness of his sins." A year or so afterwards the young bard of Ammanford was preaching with me at the anniversary services of Maesybar Chapel, Llansamlet. In the course of conversation I discovered, that he was inclined to look upon Mr. Herbert as the entertainer of eccentric notions, not having come into close personal contact with him. I strongly urged him to seek Mr. Herbert, simply to hear the wonderful story of his conversion to listen without controversy or gainsaying. Imagine, therefore, my joy when I read in your paper this morning that in his teaching and preaching This young and able minister gives prominence to "assurance of forgiveness," the distinctive tenet in the creed of my friend Herbert.

This does not necessarily mean that, no one can be saved without attaining this assurance, but it does mean that all Christians should strive for its attainment, and that without it all effort at the evangelisation of the country is feeble and half-hearted, with it conversion is only half completed. To Mr. Nantllais Williams I, therefore, say, "Go on, preach forgiveness on the part of God and assurance of forgiveness on the part of man, for that is the law and the prophets, that is the Bible and the Creed, that is the Gospel and the Confession of Faith." I say this to prevent any misunderstanding on the part of the Calvinistic Methodists of Ammanford respecting the teaching of their pastor, and they will, I believe, acknowledge that I ought to know something about the theology of our connexion. My only excuse for this reference is to remove all hindrances from the way of our young ministers, who seem to strive after the higher life, and whose spirits are baptised "with the Holy Ghost and with fire."

Cerdd yn mlaen, nefol dan,
Cymmer yma feddiant glan

P.S This does not mean approval of the unseemly interruption which, according to your report, a good lady occasioned by asking the preacher for the day 'if he was truly saved.' Indiscretions of this kind occasion much harm. She ought to have taken for granted that he, as a servant of Christ, was truly saved.

Printed in Great Britain
by Amazon

35268520R00068